FIELD GUIDES

SNAKES

Carol Hand

Abdo Reference

An Imprint of Abdo Publishing | abdobooks.com

CONTENTS

What Are Snakes? 4
How to Use This Book 6

Blind Snakes and Thread Snakes
Brahminy Blind Snake 8
Hook-Snouted Thread Snake 9
Schlegel's Giant Blind Snake 10
Texas Thread Snake 11

Heavy-Bodied Constrictors
Ball Python 12
Boa Constrictor 13
Burmese Python 14
Emerald Tree Boa 15
Green Anaconda 16
Green Tree Python 17
Reticulated Python 18
Rubber Boa 19

Pipe Snakes and Shield-Tailed Snakes
Bombay Shield-Tail 20
Red-Tailed Pipe Snake 21

File Snakes
Arafura File Snake 22
Dragon Snake 23

Colubroids: Nonvenomous Colubrids
Beauty Snake 24
California King Snake 25
California Mountain King Snake 26
Corn Snake 27
Eastern Milk Snake 28
Eastern Rat Snake 29
Egg-Eating Snake 30
Gopher Snake 31
Leaf-Nosed Snake 32
Shovel-Nosed Snake 33

Colubroids: Racers and Whip Snakes
Aesculapian Snake 34
Caspian Whip Snake 35
Coachwhip 36
Eastern Indigo Snake 37
Long-Tailed False Coral Snake 38
Racer 39

Colubroids: Garter and Water Snakes
Common Garter Snake 40
Common Grass Snake 41
Common Water Snake 42
Graham's Crayfish Snake 43
Red-Bellied Mud Snake 44
Western Ribbon Snake 45

Colubroids: Rear-Fanged Water Snakes
Crab Eater 46
Puff-Faced Water Snake 47
Tentacled Snake 48
Tiger Keelback 49

Colubroids: Goo-Eaters
Catesby's Snail-Eater 50
Coffee-Bean Snake 51
Dekay's Brown Snake 52
Northern Cat-Eyed Snake 53
Ring-Necked Snake 54
Variegated False Coral Snake 55

Colubroids: Tree Snakes and Vine Snakes

Blunt-Headed Tree Snake.................56
Boomslang 57
Brown Tree Snake 58
False Tree Coral Snake.....................59
Green Vine Snake............................ 60
Long-Nosed Tree Snake....................61
Oriental Whip Snake 62
Paradise Flying Snake 63

Vipers: Non-Pit Vipers

Adder 64
African Bush Viper 65
Desert Horned Viper......................... 66
Fea's Viper..67
Gaboon Viper 68
Puff Adder 69
Russell's Viper..................................70
Saw-Scaled Viper.............................. 71

Vipers: Pit Vipers

Bushmaster 72
Common Lancehead.......................... 73
Copperhead...................................... 74
Eastern Diamondback Rattlesnake 75
Eyelash Viper 76
Jumping Pit Viper 77
Northern Cottonmouth......................78
Pygmy Rattlesnake............................79
Sidewinder 80

Timber Rattlesnake............................81
Wagler's Pit Viper.............................82
Western Diamondback Rattlesnake 83

Terrestrial Elapoids

Amazonian Coral Snake 84
Banded Krait.....................................85
Black Mamba 86
Blue Malaysian Coral Snake.............87
Desert Death Adder.......................... 88
Eastern Bandy-Bandy....................... 89
Eastern Coral Snake......................... 90
Egyptian Cobra.................................91
Indian Cobra 92
Inland Taipan....................................93
King Brown Snake.............................94
King Cobra..95
Many-Banded Krait 96
Mozambique Spitting Cobra 97
Sand Racer....................................... 98
Sonoran Coral Snake........................ 99
Stiletto Snake 100
Tiger Snake.....................................101

Marine Elapoids

Banded Sea Krait............................ 102
Elegant Sea Snake.......................... 103
Olive-Brown Sea Snake 104
Short-Nosed Sea Snake 105
Small-Headed Sea Snake 106
Yellow-Bellied Sea Snake................ 107

Glossary..108
To Learn More..109
Photo Credits 110

WHAT ARE SNAKES?

Most people are either fascinated by or terrified of snakes. A snake's lack of limbs, curvy movement, and flicking tongue frighten many people. But most snakes are not venomous. Even fewer are deadly. Up to 138,000 people worldwide die of snakebites each year. But nearly ten times that many die in car accidents. There are approximately 3,700 snake species in the world. Of these, about 600 species are venomous. Only 200 are venomous enough to kill or seriously harm humans.

Snakes live around the world. However, there are no native snakes in Antarctica, Iceland, Greenland, Ireland, or New Zealand. Snakes live in forests, swamps, grasslands, and deserts. Some snakes live in fresh water or oceans. Some of these creatures are invasive. That means they live in areas where they are not native. Invasive species often have no predators. They can take over an area.

WHAT FEATURES DO SNAKES HAVE?

Snakes differ in size and color. They also have distinct behaviors and food habits. But all snakes have certain things in common:

- They lack limbs, external ear openings, and eyelids.

- They are ectothermic. That means a snake cannot regulate its own body temperature. It must use the environment to do so. For example, a snake can bask in the sun to warm up. It can go in the shade to cool down.

- They have scales. Scales trap moisture and reduce friction when a snake moves.

- Snakes flick their forked tongues to collect odors in the air. They identify those odors using organs on the roofs of their mouths.

- The two sides of their upper and lower jaws are not connected. Instead, they have ligaments that stretch, helping snakes open their mouths very widely. Each jaw piece can move independently to pull large prey into the snake's mouth.

WHERE DID SNAKES COME FROM?

Snakes are part of a group of vertebrates known as reptiles. Reptiles also include alligators, crocodiles, turtles, and lizards. The now-extinct dinosaurs were reptiles.

The earliest known snakes lived 167 to 140 million years ago. Their fossils have been found in England, Portugal, and the United States. Some of these early snakes had small limbs.

WHAT ROLE DO SNAKES PLAY?

Snakes play important roles in their ecosystems. They feed on many kinds of animals. Snakes are also prey for some animals, including eagles, hawks, foxes, and other snakes. Snakes help maintain Earth's biodiversity. When they are lost from food webs, ecosystems are damaged and sometimes destroyed.

Snakes control pest populations, particularly rodents. Rodents can cause many human diseases. Keeping rodent populations down helps control some diseases. Rodents, especially rats and mice, also eat many tons of food grain every year. When snakes control rodent populations, much less food is destroyed. This helps farmers and consumers.

Snake populations are declining globally. They are threatened by habitat loss, climate change, diseases, and the introduction of invasive species. Sometimes people kill snakes just because they hate and fear them. Because of the great value snakes have to the world's ecosystems, it is vital to understand and protect them.

HOW TO USE THIS BOOK

Tab shows the snake category.

VIPERS: PIT VIPERS

WAGLER'S PIT VIPER
(TROPIDOLAEMUS WAGLERI)

The snake's common name appears here.

Wagler's pit viper is a tropical snake. It once had a wide range, but due to deforestation, it is limited to areas of rain forest. Wagler's pit viper is a venomous species. It is highly arboreal. Females are larger than males. Males and juveniles are green with yellow markings. They have a red stripe through each eye. Females are black with yellow bands and green markings. They also have yellow on their faces.

FUN FACT
A Buddhist temple in Penang, Malaysia, is known as the Snake Temple. Wagler's pit vipers from the surrounding jungle shelter in the temple, which is now a tourist site.

Female

Fun Facts give interesting information related to the snake.

Male or juvenile

HOW TO SPOT

Length: Males 1.7 feet (0.5 m); females 3 feet (0.9 m)
Range: Southeast Asia including Thailand and Malaysia, the Indonesian island of Sumatra, and neighboring islands
Habitat: Tropical forests, islands and coasts, and mangrove forests
Diet: Mostly birds and ... on lizards and frogs

How to Spot features give information on how to identify the snake.

WESTERN DIAMONDBACK RATTLESNAKE *(CROTALUS ATROX)*

The western diamondback rattlesnake is one of several rattlesnakes in the southwestern United States. The snake is large and highly venomous. It can be gray, brown, reddish, or yellowish. It has a pattern of diamonds with white chevrons between them. The tail has distinct black and white rings. It has become rare in some areas, with many being killed in annual rattlesnake roundups. The western diamondback is aggressive. It stands its ground and may strike when threatened.

HOW TO SPOT

Length: 4 to 6 feet (1.2 to 1.8 m)
Range: Southwestern United States and northern Mexico
Habitat: Lowland floodplains, rocky canyons, wooded hillsides, semideserts, and farmlands
Diet: Birds, lizards, and small mammals as large as jackrabbits

RATTLESNAKE ROUNDUPS

Snakes are often killed needlessly out of fear and cruelty. In rattlesnake roundups, tens of thousands of rattlesnakes per year are captured and killed. Hunters are paid for bringing in rattlesnakes. They often pour gasoline into tortoise dens to force out rattlesnakes. This pollutes the area and harms hundreds of other species.

83

The snake's scientific name appears here.

This paragraph provides information about the snake.

Images show the snake.

Sidebars provide additional information about the topic.

7

BLIND SNAKES AND THREAD SNAKES

BRAHMINY BLIND SNAKE
(INDOTYPHLOPS BRAMINUS)

The brahminy blind snake is from Southeast Asia, India, and Sri Lanka. This snake is shiny and smooth. It is dark brown or black with a rounded head and tiny eyes. It is nonvenomous. All brahminy blind snakes are female. It is the only snake that must reproduce by parthenogenesis. This means the female's eggs are not fertilized. Instead, they hatch into clones of the mother. The snake colonizes new habitats easily because only one snake is needed start a new colony.

HOW TO SPOT

Length: 4.4 to 6.5 inches (11.2 to 16.5 cm)
Range: Native to India, Sri Lanka, and Southeast Asia; introduced worldwide
Habitat: A variety of habitats, including coastal ports, gardens, and nurseries
Diet: Larvae and eggs of termites and ants

The brahminy blind snake turns blue when it is about to shed its skin.

FUN FACT
The brahminy blind snake is sometimes called the flowerpot snake. This is because it hides in the soil of potted plants and crops. It has hitched rides around the world by doing this.

HOOK-SNOUTED THREAD SNAKE *(MYRIOPHOLIS MACRORHYNCHA)*

The hook-snouted thread snake is nonvenomous and oviparous. It is a long, thin snake. Its head ends in a downturned hook nose. It has two distinct color patterns. The African morph is solid brown. The Asian morph is a translucent pink. The Asian snake's scales have so little pigment that its internal organs are visible.

HOW TO SPOT

Length: 8.9 to 9 inches (22.6 to 22.9 cm)
Range: North Africa and Western Asia
Habitat: Farm fields with loose soil, and forests
Diet: Ants and ant larvae

TYPES OF REPRODUCTION

Most snakes reproduce by laying eggs. They are oviparous. But many snakes are viviparous. They produce shell-less eggs that develop inside the snakes' bodies. The young are born live, hatching out of the membrane.

BLIND SNAKES AND THREAD SNAKES

SCHLEGEL'S GIANT BLIND SNAKE *(AFROTYPHLOPS SCHLEGELII)*

Scientists believe Schlegel's giant blind snake is the world's largest species of blind snake. Like all blind snakes, it is a burrower. However, it tunnels deeper than its smaller relatives. This snake comes to the surface at night after heavy rains. Schlegel's giant blind snake has a hooked beak that helps it burrow into termite mounds, which provide shelter and food. These snakes usually have yellow, yellow-brown, or blue-gray backs with dark spots.

FUN FACT
Blind snakes and thread snakes have very tiny eyes and smooth, shiny scales. They are all burrowers.

HOW TO SPOT
Length: 2 to 3 feet (0.6 to 0.9 m)
Range: Southern Africa, including southern Angola, Namibia, Botswana, Mozambique, and South Africa
Habitat: Coastal forests, and grasslands and savannas
Diet: Termites and termite larvae

TEXAS THREAD SNAKE
(RENA DULCIS)

The Texas thread snake is solid pinkish brown with a silvery shine. It has a tiny mouth and tiny eyes. It wriggles through loose soil or follows tracks made by earthworms or ants. To avoid being attacked by ants, it releases feces and a nasty chemical. When it coats itself by rolling in this mixture, ants leave it alone. Then the snake is free to feed on their young.

HOW TO SPOT

Length: 5 to 11.8 inches (12.7 to 30 cm)
Range: Southwestern United States and Mexico
Habitat: Oak-juniper woodlands, dry grasslands, and semideserts
Diet: Termites and ants

FUN FACT
Screech owls sometimes take live Texas thread snakes into their nests. The snakes eat insects that would harm the owlets.

HEAVY-BODIED CONSTRICTORS

BALL PYTHON *(PYTHON REGIUS)*

The ball python is one of the smallest African pythons. It is short and thick. This snake is dark brown or black with pale-brown saddles on its back. A light stripe runs across the eye from the snout to the back of the head. Ball pythons live in burrows and come out at night to hunt. The ball python is named for its defensive posture. It curls up in a ball with its head in the middle. It is gentle and a popular pet.

HOW TO SPOT

Length: 3.3 to 4.9 feet (1 to 1.5 m)
Range: West and Central Africa
Habitat: Scrublands and open or wooded savannas
Diet: Small mammals

Typical and albino ball python colorations

ALBINO BALL PYTHON

The albino ball python has no dark pigments. It is pure white with a bright-yellow pattern and pink or red eyes. This is a result of a genetic mutation. Albinos are rare in the wild, but they have been bred in captivity and are popular with pet owners.

BOA CONSTRICTOR
(BOA CONSTRICTOR)

Like all constrictors, the boa constrictor has small, hooked teeth to grab and hold its prey while squeezing it to death. It is gray or brown with dark-brown saddles on its back and sides. Boa constrictors are viviparous. A female gives birth to around 60 live babies, each up to 2 feet (0.6 m) long. The snake has a prehensile tail and is comfortable in trees or on the ground but is also a good swimmer. It often lives in abandoned animal burrows.

FUN FACT
All boas have hind leg remnants called pelvic spurs. The spurs are larger in males and are used in courtship.

HOW TO SPOT

Length: 6.6 to 9.8 feet (2 to 3 m)
Range: Mexico, Central America, and South America
Habitat: Rain forests, grasslands, farmlands and other human habitats, islands, and semideserts
Diet: Birds, lizards, and mammals including dogs, porcupines, vampire bats, deer, and opossums

HEAVY-BODIED CONSTRICTORS

BURMESE PYTHON
(PYTHON BIVITTATUS)

The Burmese python is one of the world's five largest snakes. It has a yellowish-brown back with brown saddles. It lives near bodies of water and is an excellent swimmer. Its ability to grasp tree branches with its prehensile tail makes it a good climber. The Burmese python is nocturnal. Like all pythons, it is nonvenomous and kills its prey by constriction. It lays large clutches of 30 to 100 eggs.

FUN FACT
Burmese pythons can weigh up to 200 pounds (91 kg) and be as big around as a telephone pole.

HOW TO SPOT
Length: 16 to 23 feet (4.9 to 7 m)
Range: Myanmar, Thailand, China, and Nepal; isolated populations on islands of Java, Bali, and Sulawesi
Habitat: Tropical dry forests, grasslands near rivers, and woodlands
Diet: Mammals ranging in size from rodents to deer, and sometimes birds

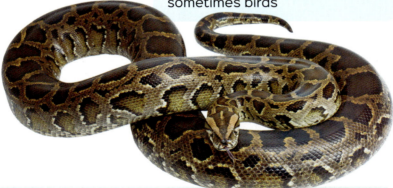

BURMESE PYTHONS IN FLORIDA
Pet owners have released Burmese pythons into the wild in Florida. These large, rapidly reproducing snakes now live and breed successfully in the Everglades. They consume most types of animals, including alligators. They have become a major threat to Florida wildlife.

EMERALD TREE BOA
(CORALLUS CANINUS)

The emerald tree boa lives in the regions north and south of the Amazon River and east of the Rio Negro in South America. This snake is bright green, usually with white bars on its back. Young emerald tree boas can be range from red to orange to brown. This snake has a muscular prehensile tail. It also has a long head. It is a nocturnal tree-dweller found in lowland rain forests.

HOW TO SPOT

Length: 4.6 to 6 feet (1.4 to 1.8 m)
Range: Northern South America
Habitat: Tropical rain forests
Diet: Lizards, birds, and small mammals, especially rodents and bats

Adult

Juvenile

EMERALD TREE BOA OR GREEN TREE PYTHON?

Emerald tree boas and green tree pythons look similar. They even have similar resting positions. But they are not closely related. When species that are not closely related have similar behaviors and appearances, it is called parallel evolution. Emerald tree boas have longer heads than green tree pythons. The markings on their backs are different too. The two species live in different parts of the world.

HEAVY-BODIED CONSTRICTORS

GREEN ANACONDA
(EUNECTES MURINUS)

The green anaconda is the world's heaviest snake. Females can weigh up to 550 pounds (250 kg). The snake is dark green with large black markings. Green anacondas are excellent swimmers. It is easier for large, heavy snakes such as anacondas to move in the water than on land. The green anaconda's eyes and nostrils are on top of its head. This allows it to see and breathe while underwater. It lies submerged at night waiting for prey.

HOW TO SPOT

Length: Males 9.8 feet (3 m) on average; females 19.7 feet (6 m) on average
Range: Most of northern South America
Habitat: Rain forest rivers, flooded savannas, and lakes
Diet: Waterbirds, caimans, and large mammals such as deer, capybaras, and tapirs

FUN FACT
Mating anacondas form what is called a breeding ball. Up to 12 male anacondas will wrap themselves around a female and attempt to mate with her. Afterward, a female will not eat for seven months until her babies are born live.

GREEN TREE PYTHON
(MORELIA VIRIDIS)

Adult green tree pythons are bright green with white or yellow stripes down the back. Young snakes are bright yellow, orange, or reddish brown. Bright colorations help the pythons blend into their rain forest habitats. This slender, muscular snake is arboreal, or tree-dwelling. It sleeps coiled and draped over tree branches. It has a large head and long teeth for trapping its prey.

Adults

Juveniles

HOW TO SPOT

Length: 3.3 to 5 feet (1 to 1.5 m)

Range: New Guinea and nearby islands, Indonesia, and the Cape York Peninsula of Australia

Habitat: Rain forests and monsoon forests

Diet: Usually small mammals such as mice and rats; sometimes birds and lizards

HEAVY-BODIED CONSTRICTORS

RETICULATED PYTHON
(PYTHON RETICULATUS)

The reticulated python is the world's longest snake and one of the three heaviest. The reticulated python has a long body. It has a net-like pattern of orange, black, white, and tan. Its head is long and sometimes yellow. A black-and-orange stripe runs down the center of the head. It is an excellent swimmer, and the reticulated python has colonized many islands within its range. The female lays up to 100 leathery eggs that stick together in a pile. She guards the eggs from predators.

HOW TO SPOT
Length: Males 20 to 23 feet (6.1 to 7 m); females 20 to 33 feet (6.1 to 10.1 m)
Range: Southeast Asia
Habitat: Forests near rivers, rain forests, and mangrove swamps
Diet: Mammals ranging in size from rodents to deer; occasionally sun bears or humans

FUN FACT
Pythons have heat-sensitive pits on the lips and the tip of the snout to sense their endothermic prey.

SNAKE JAWS AND GIANT PREY
A snake's lower jaws are not permanently attached to each other. They're connected by an elastic ligament, which lets them expand and move independently. The same is true of upper jaws. One part of the jaw moves forward, pulling part of the prey into the snake's mouth. Teeth in the other parts of the jaw hold on to the prey. This process continues until the prey is consumed.

RUBBER BOA *(CHARINA BOTTAE)*

The rubber boa is the northernmost boa in the world. It is gray, brown, olive brown, pinkish, or green, with no markings. Its sides and belly are light yellow. The rubber boa has a rounded head and stumpy tail. It stalks prey before striking and killing by constriction. It has adapted to many habitats but dislikes heat. It tends to stay in cool, moist areas such as rodent burrows or under rocks or logs.

HOW TO SPOT

Length: 1.3 to 2.1 feet (0.4 to 0.6 m)

Range: Northwestern United States to British Columbia, Canada; isolated populations in Southern California

Habitat: Woodlands, desert edges, grasslands, and evergreen or pine-oak forests

Diet: Lizards, salamanders, small mammals such as rodents and moles, and birds; juveniles eat reptile eggs and lizards

HOW CONSTRICTORS KILL

People once thought constrictors broke their prey's bones or suffocated them. But a study of boas showed that constriction kills by cutting off the blood supply to the brain. After death, the constrictor then ingests its prey whole, like nearly all snakes.

PIPE SNAKES AND SHIELD-TAILED SNAKES

BOMBAY SHIELD-TAIL
(UROPELTIS MACROLEPIS)

The Bombay shield-tail is a small snake. It protects itself from predators by burrowing into the ground. Its shield tail aids in this. The tail looks as though it has been cut off at an angle. This scale-covered end makes a shield that the snake uses to block its burrow behind it. When their burrows flood during monsoon season, Bombay shield-tails come to the surface. The snake has a stout body with large, iridescent black scales. The sides have yellowish bars or spots that may form a stripe under the throat.

HOW TO SPOT

Length: 11.8 to 12.8 inches (30 to 32.5 cm)
Range: Southwestern India
Habitat: Forests
Diet: Earthworms and other soft invertebrates

RED-TAILED PIPE SNAKE
(CYLINDROPHIS RUFFUS)

The red-tailed pipe snake is a burrower. Its cylindrical body is well-suited for pushing through leaf litter and soft soil. It is also a good swimmer. It has a short, blunt head and a tail with reddish stripes. Its body is dark and iridescent with reddish bands, including one on the back of the neck. The red-tailed pipe snake is viviparous.

HOW TO SPOT

Length: 2.3 to 3 feet (0.7 to 0.9 m)

Range: South China, Java, Borneo, Sulawesi, and Southeast Asia, including Laos, Thailand, Myanmar, Vietnam, and Cambodia

Habitat: Lowland rain forests, swamps, rice paddies, and saltwater lagoons

Diet: Snakes and caecilians (wormlike amphibians)

FUN FACT
When threatened, the red-tailed pipe snake hides its head in the middle of its coils, displaying the red on its tail. This may scare predators away or confuse them.

FILE SNAKES

ARAFURA FILE SNAKE
(ACROCHORDUS ARAFURAE)

The Arafura file snake is slow-moving, nocturnal, and completely aquatic. Females are larger than males, and the snake is viviparous. The Arafura file snake has baggy skin that is mostly light brown or gray. It has a darker, net-like pattern on its back. The snake lives entirely in water, but its preferred habitat varies with the season. In the dry season, it seeks out backwater lagoons and stagnant pools in rivers called billabongs. During the wet season, it migrates to flooded grasslands.

HOW TO SPOT

Length: Males 3.3 to 4 feet (1 to 1.2 m); females 4.6 to 5.6 feet (1.4 to 1.7 m)
Range: Northern Australia and southern New Guinea
Habitat: Still or slow-moving water bodies, including freshwater lagoons, creeks, billabongs, and rivers
Diet: Fish

FUN FACT
Aboriginal Australians hunt Arafura file snakes for food. Women wade into the river and feel for the snakes under submerged logs.

DRAGON SNAKE
(XENODERMUS JAVANICUS)

The dragon snake is named for its rows of keeled scales that cause it to resemble a dragon. There are three rows down the back and one on each side. The other scales are very small. The snake is long and slender. It has dark-gray coloring on its back and off-white on its belly. It is nocturnal and not often seen. It rests under logs during the day and comes out at night to hunt frogs in rain forest leaf litter.

HOW TO SPOT

Length: Around 2 feet (0.6 m)
Range: Southeast Asia, including Myanmar, Thailand, Malaysia, Indonesia, Java, Sumatra, and Borneo
Habitat: Lowland rain forests and rice paddies
Diet: Frogs, tadpoles, small fish

COLUBROIDS: NONVENOMOUS COLUBRIDS

BEAUTY SNAKE *(ELAPHE TAENIURA)*

The beauty snake is also called the beauty rat snake. They are grayish brown, yellowish brown, or olive. Their skin also has a black chain-like pattern. Beauty snakes are widely distributed in southern Asia. In some areas, they live in limestone caves, where they are known as cave racers. They feed on bats and small birds called cave swiftlets. In the open, this species eats small mammals and birds. Beauty snakes are nonvenomous. They kill by constriction.

HOW TO SPOT

Length: 4.3 to 8.2 feet (1.3 to 2.5 m)

Range: China, Taiwan, Bhutan, northeast India, Ryukyu Islands, Myanmar, Vietnam, Thailand, Laos, Borneo, Sumatra, and Malaysia

Habitat: Rain forests, mountain forests, limestone caves, rice paddies, and human habitats

Diet: Various birds and small mammals, including bats

CALIFORNIA KING SNAKE
(LAMPROPELTIS CALIFORNIAE)

The California king snake is a powerful constrictor. It will eat almost any animal it can overpower. It is a smooth snake with a long tail, rounded head, and large eyes. Coastal varieties are brown with cream bands or a stripe down the back. Desert varieties are black with white bands. It is a common pet.

Banded morph

FUN FACT
All king snakes and milk snakes are oviparous, laying small clutches of one to 24 eggs, depending on the species.

HOW TO SPOT

Length: 2.6 to 3.9 feet (0.8 to 1.2 m)
Range: Southern Oregon through Baja California and Sonora, Mexico
Habitat: Deserts, semideserts, grasslands, farming areas, canyons, and wetlands
Diet: Varied, including frogs, salamanders, other snakes, birds, small mammals, and large insects; also turtle and bird eggs

Striped morph

THE KING OF SNAKES
King snakes are considered the "king" of snakes because they eat other snakes, including rattlesnakes, cottonmouths, and copperheads. King snakes are active hunters that seek out their prey. They have a natural resistance to viper venom, allowing them to safely hunt these venomous snakes.

COLUBROIDS: NONVENOMOUS COLUBRIDS

CALIFORNIA MOUNTAIN KING SNAKE *(LAMPROPELTIS ZONATA)*

California mountain king snakes are found in western North America. The snake adapts to a wide variety of habitats and feeds on many animals. It is smooth and slender. The snake has a short tail and a narrow head. The body has wide red bands between narrow black bands, with white or cream in between. These brightly colored bands cause predators to mistake the California mountain king snake for the venomous coral snake. The predators often avoid preying on the king snake as a result.

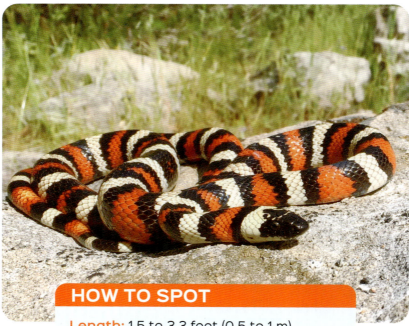

HOW TO SPOT

Length: 1.5 to 3.3 feet (0.5 to 1 m)
Range: Western United States and northwestern Mexico
Habitat: Forests, woodlands near rivers, slopes of rocky canyons, and chaparral
Diet: Lizards, small snakes, small mammals and birds, and eggs

CORN SNAKE *(PANTHEROPHIS GUTTATUS)*

The corn snake is usually orange or brownish yellow. It has dark-red saddle-shaped markings outlined in black on its back. The name *corn snake* comes from the checkerboard pattern of black and white on its underside, which resembles multicolored flint corn. Corn snakes usually live in forests. They also tolerate human habitations such as old buildings, barns, and even homes, where they search for rodents. They spend most of their time underground in animal burrows or hidden under logs or boards. They are good climbers.

HOW TO SPOT

Length: 2 to 5.9 feet (0.6 to 1.8 m)

Range: United States from New Jersey to Florida, and west to Texas

Habitat: Hardwood forests, pine barrens, swamps, and near human habitations

Diet: Rodents, birds, and eggs; will also eat frogs, lizards, and snakes

FUN FACT
Corn snakes are sometimes mistaken for copperheads, which are venomous. But copperheads have hourglass-shaped blotches on their backs rather than saddle-shaped ones.

COLUBROIDS: NONVENOMOUS COLUBRIDS

EASTERN MILK SNAKE
(LAMPROPELTIS TRIANGULUM)

The eastern milk snake is not venomous, but it is a powerful constrictor. It is gray or cream-colored with red, orange, or brown dorsal saddles with black edges. It has a narrow head. When alarmed, the eastern milk snake vibrates its tail. When it's in dead leaves, the vibrations make a rattling sound. This is the same warning method used by rattlesnakes, so the sound can confuse predators. The eastern milk snake often hides under rocks, logs, or boards. It also burrows and spends much of its time underground.

HOW TO SPOT

Length: 1.3 to 5.9 feet (0.4 to 1.8 m)
Range: Southeastern Canada and eastern United States
Habitat: Rocky hillsides, woodlands, floodplains, scrublands, and marsh edges
Diet: Amphibians, small snakes, small mammals, birds, eggs, and invertebrates

FUN FACT

The milk snake's name comes from an old myth that milk snakes suck the milk from cows' udders. The myth exists because they were often found in barns, but they actually fed on rodents there.

EASTERN RAT SNAKE
(PANTHEROPHIS ALLEGHANIENSIS)

The eastern rat snake is a good climber. It is able to climb even very smooth tree trunks. An eastern rat snake's appearance changes depending on where it lives. Eastern rat snakes living in the northern parts of their range are black with faint stripes. Populations in their central range are gray with black blotches or nearly pure black. Southern populations also vary in color. They can be yellowish gray, orange, or tan with brown stripes or blotches. Across the range, juveniles are gray with very dark blotches on the back.

HOW TO SPOT

Length: 3.3 to 6 feet (1 to 1.8 m)
Range: United States, from New England to the Florida Keys and west to Kansas, Oklahoma, and Texas
Habitat: Farmlands and many woodland habitats
Diet: Mammals, birds, frogs, lizards, and snakes

FUN FACT
The eastern rat snake sometimes eats chickens or their eggs, resulting in the nickname "chicken snake."

COLUBROIDS: NONVENOMOUS COLUBRIDS

EGG-EATING SNAKE
(DASYPELTIS SCABRA)

Egg-eating snakes are gray or light brown with dark-brown or black saddles. The belly is white with gray or black speckles or splotches. There are usually one or two V-shaped markings on the top of the head. Egg-eating snakes can open their mouths wide. This allows them to swallow very large bird eggs. After swallowing, a ridge on the underside of the backbone helps break the eggshell. The snake swallows the egg's contents and regurgitates the shell. The egg-eating snake is a mimic of the venomous saw-scaled viper. However, egg-eating snakes are harmless.

HOW TO SPOT

Length: 1.8 to 3.3 feet (0.6 to 1 m)
Range: Southern and eastern Africa, into Saudi Arabia and Yemen
Habitat: Savannas and grasslands
Diet: Eggs

GOPHER SNAKE *(PITUOPHIS CATENIFER)*

The gopher snake is widespread in the United States. It can adapt to a variety of habitats. It is usually tan or light gray with many dark-brown or red blotches. The underside is lighter, and there are dark blotches along the sides. The gopher snake hunts prey in burrows or rocky crevices. It is preyed upon by hawks, foxes, and coyotes. When in danger, the gopher snake coils up, vibrates its tail, and hisses loudly. It also flattens its head, increasing its resemblance to a venomous rattlesnake.

FUN FACT
The gopher snake can make a loud hissing sound that sounds like a rattlesnake's rattle. The gopher snake fills its lungs with air and forces the air over a piece of cartilage in its windpipe.

HOW TO SPOT

Length: 5.9 to 9.2 feet (1.8 to 2.8 m)
Range: Southwestern Canada; southern, western, and central United States, into central Mexico
Habitat: Forests and woodlands, prairies, deserts, semideserts, and farmlands
Diet: Mostly mammals, also lizards, birds, and bird eggs

COLUBROIDS: NONVENOMOUS COLUBRIDS

LEAF-NOSED SNAKE
(PHYLLORHYNCHUS DECURTATUS)

The small leaf-nosed snake is pale tan, pink, or grayish, with dark-brown blotches. The underside is plain white. The leaf-nosed snake is named for the scale on its nose. The scale is large and raised above the others. It looks like a folded leaf. This scale may help the snake dig in the sand for prey. Leaf-nosed snakes are nocturnal and not often seen, but they may be spotted on roads at night. The snake is harmless, but it may strike if threatened.

FUN FACT
Though leaf-nosed snakes eat eggs, they usually do not eat them whole. Instead, they use their teeth to cut slits in the leathery eggshells. Then they drink the egg's contents.

HOW TO SPOT
Length: 1 to 1.7 feet (0.3 to 0.5 m)
Range: Southern California, Utah, Arizona, southern Nevada, northern Baja California, and the western edge of Mexico
Habitat: Sandy or gravelly deserts, open flats, seasonal creeks, and foothills
Diet: Leathery-shelled eggs of lizards and snakes

SHOVEL-NOSED SNAKE
(CHIONACTIS OCCIPITALIS)

The harmless shovel-nosed snake is smooth and shiny. Its head is narrow. A single, large, spade-like scale sits on the tip of its nose. Its body is cream-colored with dark-brown bands that usually do not entirely circle the snake. It is nocturnal, burrowing underground in the daytime. Shovel-nosed snakes can move under the surface of the sand, covering great distances without surfacing. They move across sand with a series of distinctive S-shaped curves in the body. They are often seen crossing roads at night.

HOW TO SPOT

Length: 0.9 to 1.4 feet (0.3 to 0.4 m)
Range: Southern California, Nevada, western Arizona, Baja California, and northern Mexico
Habitat: Dry deserts with loose sand and little vegetation
Diet: Invertebrates, including insects and larvae, scorpions, spiders, and centipedes

COLUBROIDS: RACERS AND WHIP SNAKES

AESCULAPIAN SNAKE
(ZAMENIS LONGISSIMUS)

The Aesculapian snake is found throughout much of Europe and western Asia. There are also introduced populations in northern Wales and the city of London. The Aesculapian snake has smooth scales and a long tail. It is a solid olive green, brown, or gray in color and is lighter on the underside. Juveniles may have a brown checkerboard pattern with a stripe behind the eye and a black-and-yellow collar.

HOW TO SPOT

Length: 4.6 to 5.2 feet (1.4 to 1.6 m), up to 7.4 feet (2.3 m)

Range: Northeast Spain, France, Italy, Germany, Poland, Czech Republic, the Balkans, Greece, Bulgaria, Romania, Ukraine, Russia, Turkey, and Iran

Habitat: Woodlands, riverbanks, and agricultural or human habitats such as vineyards, orchards, and dry stone walls

Diet: Rodents and birds; juveniles eat mice and lizards

FUN FACT
The Aesculapian snake is named for Asclepius, the Greek god of medicine. It is used on the Rod of Asclepius, the symbol of medicine.

CASPIAN WHIP SNAKE
(DOLICHOPHIS CASPIUS)

The Caspian whip snake has an olive-green, olive-brown, or gray back. Each scale is outlined in black, giving it a net-like appearance. The underside is yellowish or pale green. When encountered, the snake tries to flee. However, if the Caspian whip snake is cornered it will defend itself by striking high and biting. Caspian whip snakes are nonvenomous.

HOW TO SPOT

Length: 6.6 to 8.2 feet (2 to 2.5 m)

Range: Throughout southeastern Europe and southwestern Russia

Habitat: Rocky hillsides, forests, grasslands, semideserts, and human habitats such as hedges, vineyards, and stone walls

Diet: Juveniles eat mostly lizards; adults also eat birds, small mammals, and other snakes

COLUBROIDS: RACERS AND WHIP SNAKES

COACHWHIP *(MASTICOPHIS FLAGELLUM)*

Coachwhips are widely distributed in the southern United States. They are among the country's longest snakes, sometimes reaching more than 8 feet (2.4 m) long. Coachwhips are slender and smooth. They have long tails and pointed snouts. This snake's color varies by location. Many populations are pale brown, others pure black, and still others bright red or pink. Often the coachwhip's color pattern appears braided, similar to a 1700s coachman's whip. These snakes are very fast. They are active in the daytime, even in hot weather.

FUN FACT
Some people believe coachwhips actively chase people, constricting and lashing them to death. This is untrue, although coachwhips will defend themselves if cornered.

HOW TO SPOT

Length: 3.3 to 5 feet (1 to 1.5 m)
Range: Throughout the southern United States and into Mexico
Habitat: Desert-like environments, prairies, woodlands, and farmlands
Diet: Reptiles and their eggs, amphibians, birds, small mammals, and insects

EASTERN INDIGO SNAKE
(DRYMARCHON COUPERI)

The eastern indigo snake was once common in the southeastern United States. Because of habitat loss, it is now one of the most endangered US snake species. These snakes are solid black with red or cream coloring on the throat and chin. As in many other snakes, females attract males by releasing pheromones. Males carry out a ritual combat dance. They twine around each other and try to force the other's head to the ground. The winner mates with the female.

HOW TO SPOT

Length: 4.9 to 6.9 feet (1.5 to 2.1 m)

Range: Southeastern United States including Florida and southern Georgia

Habitat: Temperate habitats including deserts, dunes, grasslands, forests, scrub forests, and marshes; also agricultural areas

Diet: Highly varied, including mammals, frogs, fish, lizards, birds, eggs, other snakes, and young turtles

COLUBROIDS: RACERS AND WHIP SNAKES

LONG-TAILED FALSE CORAL SNAKE (SCAPHIODONTOPHIS ANNULATUS)

The long-tailed false coral snake has many common names, including neckband snake or half coral snake. These names come from its unique pattern. The head end is brightly colored, usually red with black and yellow or white bands. The body and tail are often solid brown. But sometimes the tail is colorfully banded like the head. Very rarely, the entire snake is banded. The snake's teeth are spatula shaped. This allows the long-tailed false coral snake to tightly grasp skinks, its favorite prey. The snake can swallow a skink in a few seconds.

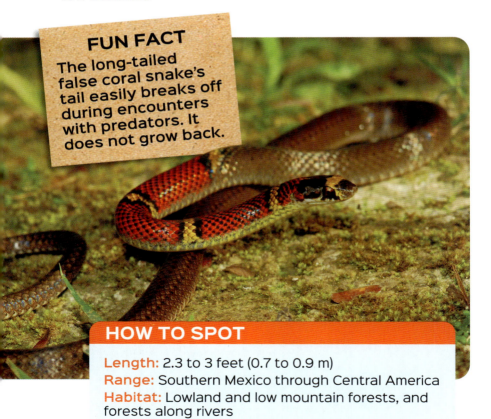

FUN FACT
The long-tailed false coral snake's tail easily breaks off during encounters with predators. It does not grow back.

HOW TO SPOT

Length: 2.3 to 3 feet (0.7 to 0.9 m)
Range: Southern Mexico through Central America
Habitat: Lowland and low mountain forests, and forests along rivers
Diet: Lizards, mostly smooth-scaled skinks

RACER *(COLUBER CONSTRICTOR)*

Despite its scientific name, the racer is not a constrictor. Instead, it presses prey to the ground or simply swallows it alive. The racer is long and thin. Adults can be solid black with a white chin and throat. They can also be brown, dull green, blue, or sometimes brown with lighter and darker blotches. Juveniles are always dull brown with dark-brown blotches down the back. The racer is nonvenomous and nonaggressive but bites when threatened.

HOW TO SPOT

Length: 3 to 6.2 feet (0.9 to 1.9 m)

Range: North America, from southern Canada through most of the United States into Mexico and Central America

Habitat: Forests and woodlands, grasslands, and swamps, often near streams

Diet: Small mammals, most kinds of reptiles and amphibians, reptile and fish eggs, spiders, and insects

COLUBROIDS: GARTER AND WATER SNAKES

COMMON GARTER SNAKE
(THAMNOPHIS SIRTALIS)

The common garter snake is widespread in North America. Its back is often olive, gray, brown, or black. Three stripes run down the snake's body. The stripes can be yellow, white, green, or brown. Western populations often have red on the sides. Common garter snakes are commonly found near permanent water sources. They live in human habitats if there are hiding places such as logs or boards. They are viviparous and can have more than 50 young at once.

HOW TO SPOT

Length: 1.5 to 4.6 feet (0.5 to 1.4 m)

Range: Southern Canada, most of the United States, and northern Mexico

Habitat: Both aquatic and terrestrial, including lakes, ponds, rivers, wooded swamps, bayous, marshes, woodlands, prairies, and grasslands

Diet: Amphibians, fish, invertebrates, earthworms, small mammals, and birds

FUN FACT
Common garter snakes are resistant to toxins from western toads and rough-skinned newts, but they may appear sluggish or intoxicated after eating them.

MANITOBA SNAKE PITS

Every year, tourists gather in the small town of Narcisse, 65 miles (105 km) north of Winnipeg, Canada. There, they witness the emergence of 70,000 common garter snakes from the Manitoba snake pits. These are large, underground limestone caverns around Narcisse. The snakes spend seven months per year hibernating in the pits.

COMMON GRASS SNAKE
(NATRIX NATRIX)

The nonvenomous common grass snake lives near ponds, lakes, canals, and ditches, and it is an excellent swimmer. The female is much larger than the male. Males are long and thin and usually no more than 1.6 feet (0.5 m) long. The snake is olive, dark green, or gray. A yellow or white collar around its neck gives it another common name, the ringed snake. It has a stout body, keeled scales, and a triangular head. It is oviparous, with females laying eight to 40 eggs.

HOW TO SPOT

Length: 2 to 3.3 feet (0.6 to 1 m)
Range: Europe and western Asia
Habitat: Damp locations near bodies of water
Diet: Frogs and toads; sometimes tadpoles, salamanders, or fish

COLUBROIDS: GARTER AND WATER SNAKES

COMMON WATER SNAKE
(NERODIA SIPEDON)

The common water snake may be tan, brown, or grayish. It has a series of square, alternating blotches of a darker color. Juveniles have brighter coloring than adults. Common water snakes sometimes avoid predators by attaching to underwater logs or plants. They can remain underwater for 1.5 hours. The snake is viviparous and has four to 99 babies. During fall and spring, common water snakes are social, coiling together at basking sites. They are solitary in hotter weather.

A common water snake with her young

HOW TO SPOT

Length: 2 to 4.6 feet (0.6 to 1.4 m)
Range: Eastern and central North America
Habitat: Still waters with open areas for basking, including rivers, streams, ponds, lakes, and marshes
Diet: Fish, amphibians, crayfish, large insects, birds, small mammals, and carrion

FUN FACT
The common water snake is sometimes confused with the northern cottonmouth. But the northern cottonmouth has bands instead of blotches.

COMMON WATER SNAKES AND HUMANS

The common water snake is highly useful to humans because it feeds on diseased and dying fish. This helps control fish populations and improves the populations' overall health. This means the snake benefits sport fishers. However, it can cause problems around fish farms and hatcheries, since fish are a major part of its diet.

GRAHAM'S CRAYFISH SNAKE
(REGINA GRAHAMII)

The small Graham's crayfish snake has a brown or yellowish-brown back and yellow-tan stripes on its sides. Some snakes also have a tan stripe down the middle of their backs. Graham's crayfish snake has a yellowish belly, usually with a central row of dark spots. Early in the warm season it may rest on tree branches above the water. In winter, it stays in crayfish burrows. It bears live young.

FUN FACT
When threatened, Graham's crayfish snake releases a foul-smelling mix of musk and feces.

HOW TO SPOT

Length: 1.6 to 2.3 feet (0.5 to 0.7 m)
Range: Midwestern United States, from Iowa and Illinois south to Texas and Louisiana
Habitat: Semiaquatic; edges of ponds and streams, bottomlands, and flooded pastures
Diet: Freshly molted crayfish, occasionally salamanders, tadpoles, frogs, and snails

COLUBROIDS: GARTER AND WATER SNAKES

RED-BELLIED MUD SNAKE
(FARANCIA ABACURA)

The red-bellied mud snake has a shiny black back. Its underside has a red-and-black checkerboard pattern. Males are smaller than females but have longer tails. The snake is highly aquatic. But it will often move long distances on land between bodies of water. Although fairly common, the mud snake is not often seen. It spends most of its time hidden in aquatic plants. Red-bellied mud snakes are oviparous.

HOW TO SPOT

Length: 3 to 3.9 feet (0.9 to 1.2 m)

Range: Southeastern United States to the Gulf Coast, including Virginia, Mississippi, Louisiana, and western Tennessee

Habitat: Wooded swamps, ponds, lakes, salty marshes, edges of rivers and streams, and brackish water

Diet: Frogs, tadpoles, aquatic salamanders such as sirens and amphiumas, and occasionally fish

FUN FACT
The red-bellied mud snake has a spine on the end of its tail. It will press this spine into a predator to try to escape.

WESTERN RIBBON SNAKE
(THAMNOPHIS PROXIMUS)

The western ribbon snake is a type of garter snake. It is black with an orange stripe on its back. It has two cream or yellow stripes on its sides. The underside is white or occasionally yellowish. It is fast and difficult to catch. To escape predators, the western ribbon snake may skim across the water. The snake migrates as the weather gets colder. It often crosses roads in late fall while migrating to its hibernation spot.

HOW TO SPOT

Length: Usually around 3 feet (0.9 m)
Range: Southern Great Lakes through the Midwest and western Mexico, with populations in southern Mexico through Costa Rica
Habitat: Water in wetland habitats where cover is available
Diet: Mostly frogs and toads, occasionally lizards and fish

COLUBROIDS: REAR-FANGED WATER SNAKES

CRAB EATER *(FORDONIA LEUCOBALIA)*

The crab eater snake is also called the crab-eating mangrove snake or white-bellied mangrove snake. It is a common snake in its range. It is venomous but not harmful to humans. The crab eater's back and sides vary in color and pattern. It can be solid brown, dark gray, yellow, orange, or white. It can also be spotted in white, yellow, or black. The snake's underside is always white.

FUN FACT

Unlike most snakes, crab eaters do not always swallow their prey whole. They remove the crab's legs and claws and eat them separately from the body.

HOW TO SPOT

Length: 2.3 feet (0.7 m)
Range: India, New Guinea, and northern Australia
Habitat: Mangrove swamps, coastal mudflats, and river estuaries
Diet: Freshly molted crabs, lobsters, and fish

PUFF-FACED WATER SNAKE
(HOMALOPSIS BUCCATA)

The nocturnal puff-faced water snake has keeled scales. It is plain brown or gray, with black-edged bands. The underside is whitish. Juveniles are darker with more distinctive bands. The puff-faced water snake has a broad head with a V shape at the back. It also has dark spots on the edges of its body. Puff-faced water snakes are almost entirely aquatic.

HOW TO SPOT

Length: Up to 3.9 feet (1.2 m)
Range: India, Bangladesh, Myanmar, Cambodia, Thailand, Malaysia, Singapore, and Indonesia
Habitat: Fresh water such as swamps, ponds, and forest streams
Diet: Small fish and frogs

COLUBROIDS: REAR-FANGED WATER SNAKES

TENTACLED SNAKE
(ERPETON TENTACULATUM)

The tentacled snake is covered in keeled scales. But its defining feature is a pair of fleshy tentacles on each side of its snout. These help the snake hunt. A tentacled snake uses its prehensile tail to attach to plants. Its body is light brown, sometimes with darker stripes. It can also be dark gray with lighter mottling. This coloration helps it blend in with plants. The snake waits quietly until a fish approaches. The snake fools the fish by using a loop of its coiled body to strike at it. This scares the fish, sending it directly toward the snake's mouth.

FUN FACT
The unique tentacles on the tentacled snake's snout sense water movement. They help the snakes locate prey by detecting vibrations of swimming fish.

HOW TO SPOT
Length: 2.5 feet (0.8 m)
Range: Vietnam, Cambodia, and southern Thailand
Habitat: Ponds, stagnant bodies of water, and slow-moving rivers
Diet: Fish

TIGER KEELBACK
(RHABDOPHIS TIGRINUS)

Tiger keelbacks are both venomous and poisonous. The snake delivers venom with its rear fangs. It delivers poison through glands on the back of its neck. When threatened, the snake arches its neck, exposing the glands. A predator that bites its neck would get a face full of poison. Tiger keelbacks eat toxic toads. The snakes store the toads' poison in their glands. The tiger keelback is green with orange and black markings. This snake's venom is very powerful, quickly overwhelming prey items.

HOW TO SPOT

Length: 2 to 3.6 feet (0.6 to 1.1 m)

Range: Eastern Russia, China, South Korea, North Korea, Japan, and Taiwan

Habitat: Varied, including rice paddies, woody hillsides, and streams

Diet: Fish, frogs, toads, tadpoles, and other snakes

DO KEELBACKS KNOW THEY'RE TOXIC?

Scientists noticed that tiger keelbacks on toad-free islands fled rather than confronting predators. A controlled experiment showed that lab-raised snakes from toad-free and toad-rich environments behaved differently. But if toxin-free snakes were fed toxic toads, they changed their behavior. Scientists believe this means tiger keelbacks know when they are poisonous.

COLUBROIDS: GOO-EATERS

CATESBY'S SNAIL-EATER
(DIPSAS CATESBYI)

Catesby's snail-eater is nocturnal and arboreal. It has rounded black spots on a dark-brown body. The head is black, and the underside is white. The eyes are large. Catesby's snail-eaters and related snakes are known as goo-eaters. That's because their diets consist almost entirely of slimy snails or slippery amphibian eggs. The skull, teeth, and head muscles of these snakes are specially adapted to handle feeding on these gooey creatures.

HOW TO SPOT

Length: 0.7 to 2 feet (0.2 to 0.6 m)
Range: Amazon region of northern South America
Habitat: Amazon and Atlantic rain forests
Diet: Mollusks, especially snails and slugs

EATING SNAILS

Goo-eaters that specialize in snails don't eat the snail shells. Instead, the snake sinks its long, sharp teeth into the snail while it is outside of its shell. Then the snake relaxes its jaw muscles. The snail retreats into its shell, pulling the snake along with it. The snake can then use its specialized jaw to pull the snail out of its shell, swallowing the snail and leaving the shell behind.

COFFEE-BEAN SNAKE (NINIA SEBAE)

The coffee-bean snake is also known as the red coffee snake. This tiny, nocturnal snake is often found on coffee plantations. It is rear-fanged and mildly venomous. Although harmless to humans, it mimics several venomous coral snakes. It has keeled scales and a long tail. It is red with narrow black partial stripes on the back. Its head is black, and the snake has a black-and-yellow collar.

FUN FACT
When startled, coffee-bean snakes produce a foul smell. They also stiffen their bodies. Some observers say the snake seems like a smelly, brightly colored pencil when it does this.

HOW TO SPOT

Length: 0.5 to 1.3 feet (0.2 to 0.4 m)
Range: Southern Mexico and most of Central America
Habitat: Dry areas, including lowland and low mountainous rain forests, dry forests, and savannas; common in pastures and coffee plantations
Diet: Snails, slugs, and earthworms

COLUBROIDS: GOO-EATERS

DEKAY'S BROWN SNAKE
(STORERIA DEKAYI)

The small, nonvenomous Dekay's brown snake is widely distributed in the eastern United States and into Central America. It lives in many habitats where water is available. It hides under logs or trash, feeding on the small, soft-bodied prey that live there. It is viviparous, producing three to 31 young at a time. It is gray or brown and has rows of dark-brown dots or thin stripes running down its back. Like many other goo-eaters, this snake extracts snails from their shells.

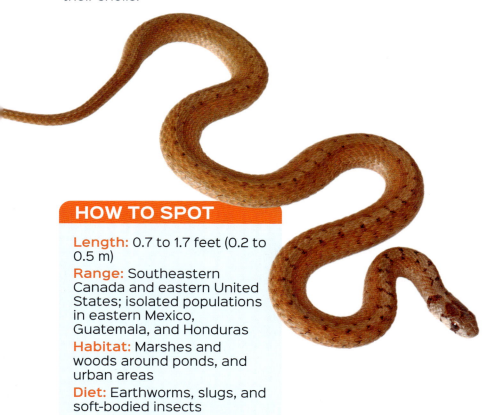

HOW TO SPOT

Length: 0.7 to 1.7 feet (0.2 to 0.5 m)

Range: Southeastern Canada and eastern United States; isolated populations in eastern Mexico, Guatemala, and Honduras

Habitat: Marshes and woods around ponds, and urban areas

Diet: Earthworms, slugs, and soft-bodied insects

NORTHERN CAT-EYED SNAKE
(LEPTODEIRA SEPTENTRIONALIS)

The northern cat-eyed snake's head is much wider than its neck. It gets its common name from its large eyes with cat-like vertical pupils. The snake's back is tan, pale gold, or pale yellow with large brown saddles. Its belly is pale orange near the head, becoming brighter toward the tail. The head has a dark, arrow-shaped marking pointing toward the tail. The snake is rear-fanged and slightly venomous.

HOW TO SPOT

Length: 1.6 to 2 feet (0.5 to 0.6 m)

Range: Southern Texas, Mexico, Central America, and South America

Habitat: Semidry scrublands and rain forests; often semidry thorny brush habitats with ponds or streams

Diet: Mostly frogs, but also lizards, toads, salamanders, small fish, and mice

A northern cat-eyed snake eats frog eggs.

FUN FACT
Some slimy prey produce a substance that glues a predator's mouth together. Goo-eaters create a substance in their mouths that counteracts this gluey substance.

COLUBROIDS: GOO-EATERS

RING-NECKED SNAKE
(DIADOPHIS PUNCTATUS)

Ring-necked snakes are widely distributed naturally. They are usually gray or blue gray on top, though sometimes they are brown or greenish gray. The underside may be red, orange, or yellow. The ring-necked snake has a ring on its neck the same color as the underside. In some areas, the snake will coil its tail into a cone shape, displaying the bright coloration on its underside. This unusual display appears to confuse some would-be predators.

HOW TO SPOT

Length: 0.8 to 2 feet (0.2 to 0.6 m)

Range: Southeastern Canada, most of the United States, and northern Mexico

Habitat: Wooded areas, rocky valleys, and railroad lines

Diet: Varied, including other snakes, salamanders, small frogs and lizards, slugs, earthworms, and insect larvae

Defensive display

FUN FACT
Ring-necked snakes can be social. They have been found in masses of more than 100 snakes.

VARIEGATED FALSE CORAL SNAKE *(PLIOCERCUS ELAPOIDES)*

The variegated false coral snake is noted for having a wide variation in its color pattern. It is rear-fanged and somewhat venomous, but it mimics several much more venomous coral snakes. Some populations of variegated false coral snake have bands in a red, yellow, black, yellow, red pattern. Others do not have the black bands. The color patterns often very closely match those of the coral snake present in its range.

HOW TO SPOT

Length: 1 to 1.6 feet (0.3 to 0.5 m)

Range: Southern Mexico through Honduras, Belize, Guatemala, and El Salvador

Habitat: Lowland areas, dry forests, low mountainous rain forests, coffee plantations, and farmlands

Diet: Frogs, salamanders, and their eggs

COLUBROIDS: TREE SNAKES AND VINE SNAKES

BLUNT-HEADED TREE SNAKE
(IMANTODES CENCHOA)

The blunt-headed tree snake has a very long, thin neck and body. It also has a large head. The snake's eyes are large with vertical pupils. The eyes project outward from the head, allowing the snake to look down. The blunt-headed tree snake's back is orange to tan, with dark-orange, red, or brown saddles edged in black along its back. These snakes are arboreal and often rest coiled up in low vegetation, such as bromeliads and coffee trees. They hunt sleeping lizards and foraging frogs on thin branches.

HOW TO SPOT

Length: 3.3 to 4.3 feet (1 to 1.3 m)

Range: Southern Mexico, Central America, and South America

Habitat: Low mountainous and lowland rain forests, dry forests if near water, and plantations

Diet: Lizards, frogs, and frog eggs

BOOMSLANG *(DISPHOLIDUS TYPUS)*

The boomslang is one of the most venomous snakes in Africa. Its venom is extremely toxic to humans, though it rarely bites unless threatened. It is slender, with a large head and very large eyes with round pupils. Adult females are olive green or brown on the back, and they are white or brown beneath. Male colors are much brighter and more variable. Their backs range from green or light blue to yellowish green with scales edged in black. Some have backs that are reddish brown or even black.

HOW TO SPOT

Length: 3.3 to 4.3 feet (1 to 1.3 m)

Range: Sub-Saharan Africa, from Senegal to Eritrea, and south to the Cape of Good Hope in South Africa

Habitat: Woody savannas, scrubby coastal areas, gardens, and hedges

Diet: Lizards, birds, and sometimes rodents or frogs

Male

FUN FACT
In 2021, a South African family found a boomslang hiding in their Christmas tree. A snake handler removed it safely.

Female

COLUBROIDS: TREE SNAKES AND VINE SNAKES

BROWN TREE SNAKE
(BOIGA IRREGULARIS)

The brown tree snake is thin with a long prehensile tail. Its head is large, and it has protruding eyes with vertical pupils. It can be gray, brown, red, orange, or yellow. Some snakes have zigzag markings on the back. Brown tree snakes are mildly venomous. They generally are not dangerous to adult humans, but bites can be more serious for babies.

HOW TO SPOT

Length: 3.3 to 9.5 feet (1 to 2.9 m)

Range: Eastern Indonesia, northern Australia and New Guinea, the Solomon Islands, and nearby archipelagos; introduced to Guam

Habitat: Rain forests, coastal forests, gardens, agricultural areas, scrublands, and near human habitations

Diet: Frogs, lizards, birds, bird eggs, small mammals, and other snakes

FUN FACT
Brown tree snakes climb poles in an interesting way. The snake wraps its tail around the pole and grabs its own body, creating a loop. Then it shimmies up the pole.

BROWN TREE SNAKES ON GUAM

The brown tree snake was accidentally introduced onto the island of Guam after World War II (1939–1945). It has since exploded to a population of more than one million. The brown tree snake has no natural predators on the island. Therefore, it is driving native birds to extinction. US officials are on constant watch to ensure that this snake is not accidentally introduced to Hawaii, where it would have similar negative effects.

FALSE TREE CORAL SNAKE
(RHINOBOTHRYUM BOVALLI)

The false tree coral snake mimics two similar coral snakes that live within its range. It is arboreal but has been seen crawling on the ground at night. It is a slender snake with a broad head and a narrow neck. It has alternating broad black and red bands with thin white bands in between. The red bands have scattered black scales. The head has large black scales rimmed in white.

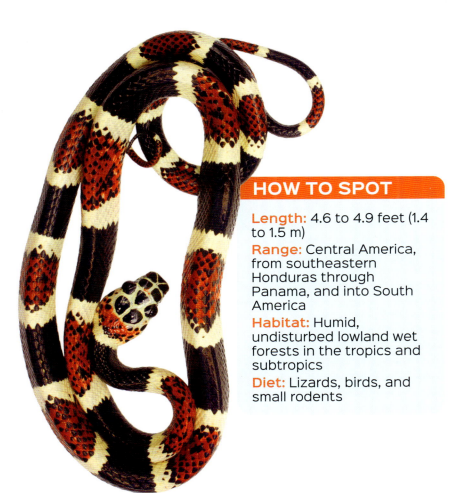

HOW TO SPOT

Length: 4.6 to 4.9 feet (1.4 to 1.5 m)

Range: Central America, from southeastern Honduras through Panama, and into South America

Habitat: Humid, undisturbed lowland wet forests in the tropics and subtropics

Diet: Lizards, birds, and small rodents

COLUBROIDS: TREE SNAKES AND VINE SNAKES

GREEN VINE SNAKE
(OXYBELIS FULGIDUS)

The green vine snake is bright emerald green, with lighter coloring on its sides and underside. The snake is slender with a long tail, and its scales are smooth. Its body is flattened, and it has a long head with a pointed snout. It sleeps among tree branches at night. It kills its prey with venom injected through its rear fangs. The venom is not dangerous to humans. When threatened, the snake adopts a distinctive pose, with its body stretched toward the intruder and the mouth opened widely.

HOW TO SPOT

Length: 4.3 to 6.6 feet (1.3 to 2 m)

Range: Southern Mexico, Central America, and South America to Bolivia

Habitat: Rain forests and forests near mountains or rivers

Diet: Birds, small mammals, frogs, and lizards

LONG-NOSED TREE SNAKE
(AHAETULLA NASUTA)

The long-nosed tree snake is slender with a long tail, long head, and long, pointed snout. Its eyes have horizontal pupils. It ranges from bright green to brown, sometimes with dark stripes on the back and a thin yellowish-green stripe on the sides. The snake hunts high in the trees. It stalks its prey using jerky movements, mimicking the way plants and trees move in the wind. It is rear-fanged with venom that kills prey but is harmless to humans.

HOW TO SPOT

Length: 5 to 6.6 feet (1.5 to 2 m)
Range: South and Southeast Asia, Indonesia, and the Philippines
Habitat: Lowland and low mountainous forests, forest edges, and gardens
Diet: Lizards and small birds

FUN FACT
The long-nosed tree snake has excellent vision. Its pupils line up with grooves down its snout. These grooves help it judge distance, similar to the sight on a rifle.

COLUBROIDS: TREE SNAKES AND VINE SNAKES

ORIENTAL WHIP SNAKE
(AHAETULLA PRASINA)

Oriental whip snakes adapt well to living in habitats developed by humans, such as gardens, parklands, wooded residential areas, and agricultural areas. The oriental whip snake is very long and thin. Its coloration ranges from light brown to dull yellowish green to bright fluorescent green. The young are born live. Oriental whip snakes have excellent vision and stalk their prey using jerky movements. They have rear-fanged venom that kills prey but does not harm humans.

FUN FACT
Oriental whip snakes can dangle over water from low branches or roots and capture small fish that come to the surface to feed.

HOW TO SPOT

Length: 5 to 6.4 feet (1.5 to 2 m)
Range: Northeast India, many Southeast Asian countries, Indonesia, and the Philippines
Habitat: Forest edges in lowlands and low mountains, and human-developed areas such as gardens
Diet: Primarily lizards and small birds; sometimes mice and frogs

PARADISE FLYING SNAKE
(CHRYSOPELEA PARADISI)

The paradise flying snake does not actually fly. Instead, it glides from tree to tree without touching the ground. It twists its body to catch air and steer. Scientists believe flying snakes glide to escape predators or hunt prey. The paradise flying snake is very slender. Scales on its back are emerald green or yellow with thick black edges, giving the snake a web-like appearance. Sometimes it has a bright line of orange or red spots down its back.

HOW TO SPOT

Length: 3.3 to 5 feet (1 to 1.5 m)
Range: Myanmar, Thailand, Singapore, Andaman Islands, Sumatra, Borneo, Java, Sulawesi, and the Philippines
Habitat: Lowland and low mountainous rain forests, and dry forests
Diet: Lizards and bats

FLYING SNAKES

The flying snake can flatten its body and form a concave shape. The snake crawls to the end of a branch, dangles in a J shape, and propels itself from the branch. It can glide long distances to the ground. It can also glide to other branches or trees. In flight, it forms an S shape. Then its flattened body forms a C shape that traps air and enables its gliding.

VIPERS: NON-PIT VIPERS

ADDER *(VIPERA BERUS)*

The adder has the widest distribution of any venomous snake, extending 125 miles (200 km) into the Arctic Circle. Males are light gray with a black zigzag pattern. Females are brown with a dark-brown zigzag. Both have a V-shaped marking on the head. The adder is viviparous. While its bite is not usually fatal to humans, it is painful and requires immediate medical attention. It can kill pets.

HOW TO SPOT

Length: 1.6 to 2.6 feet (0.5 to 0.8 m)

Range: British Isles, Northern Europe (especially Scandinavia), east through Siberia, Kazakhstan, Mongolia, and far-eastern Russia

Habitat: Highly varied, including shrubby land on poor soil, woods, farmlands, and coastal cliffs

Diet: Voles, mice, and occasionally birds; juveniles eat lizards

FUN FACT

Some European folklore says that adders can bring change to those who ask for it. A person might make a wish to shed something negative just as an adder sheds its skin.

WHAT IS A VIPER?

Vipers are one of two major families of venomous snakes. The others are elapids. Vipers' fangs are long, hollow, and hinged. When not in use, the fangs fold against the roof of the snake's mouth. They are connected to venom glands. Venom fills the fangs and is injected when the snake bites.

AFRICAN BUSH VIPER
(ATHERIS HISPIDA)

The African bush viper is also called the rough-scaled or spiny bush viper because of its keeled dorsal scales. The scales are longest on the head, giving the snake a shaggy or bristly appearance. The snake can be green, olive, bluish, or brownish with a lighter underside. It is highly arboreal and a good climber. It spends its days basking on flowering plants or reeds near rivers, where its camouflage makes it extraordinarily difficult to find.

HOW TO SPOT

Length: 2 to 2.3 feet (0.6 to 0.7 m)

Range: Countries surrounding Lake Victoria (Uganda, Rwanda, Kenya, and Tanzania) and west into the Democratic Republic of the Congo

Habitat: Rain forests, thorn forests, papyrus, and reedbeds along rivers

Diet: Lizards, frogs, young birds, and snails

VIPERS: NON-PIT VIPERS

DESERT HORNED VIPER
(CERASTES CERASTES)

The desert horned viper is short and thick, with a body like a flattened cylinder. Its head is broad and flat with keeled scales. The desert horned viper has a pair of horn-like scales behind its eyes. Its back is shades of yellow, brown, red, or gray with darker patches to match the color of the surrounding soil. Its venom contains 13 toxins and causes serious illness, though it is not usually fatal to humans.

HOW TO SPOT

Length: 1 to 3 feet (0.3 to 0.9 m)

Range: Across North Africa, especially between Egypt and Morocco, east to southwestern Saudi Arabia and Israel, and south to Mali, Niger, Chad, Sudan, and Mauritania

Habitat: Sahara Desert in rocky hills, sandy deserts, dunes, and valleys

Diet: Small rodents such as mice and voles, geckos and other lizards, and birds

FUN FACT
The desert horned viper uses a shuffling motion to submerge its body in sand. Its head stays at the surface in case a prey item wanders close by.

SIDEWINDER LOCOMOTION

Some desert vipers move by sidewinding. To sidewind, a snake lifts a loop of its body and moves it sideways. The other parts of the body bend from side to side to move the snake forward. The result is a snake that moves at an angle, not in the direction that the head is facing. Sidewinding enables the snake to move across soft desert sands.

FEA'S VIPER (AZEMIOPS FEAE)

Fea's viper does not look at all like other vipers. It has smooth scales on the body and large scales on the head. Unlike most vipers, Fea's viper lays eggs. It is active on cool, rainy nights, crawling through leaf litter in bamboo and tree fern thickets. It rests in streams and in holes in outcroppings. Fea's viper is dark gray with narrow, bright-orange bars. Its head is white or yellow with a black arrow-shaped marking on top.

HOW TO SPOT

Length: 2.3 to 3.3 feet (0.7 to 1 m)
Range: Southern China, Vietnam, and northern Myanmar
Habitat: Various types of moist forests
Diet: Small mammals, primarily shrews and rodents

VIPERS: NON-PIT VIPERS

GABOON VIPER *(BITIS GABONICA)*

The Gaboon viper is the largest African viper. It can reach more than 6 feet (1.8 m) in length and weigh more than 45 pounds (20 kg). This viper can hold the largest amount of venom in its glands of all venomous snakes. Its bite can be fatal, but it rarely bites humans. The Gaboon viper blends into leaf litter with its pattern of pastel brown, gray, purple, pink, and cream. Its head resembles a leaf.

HOW TO SPOT

Length: 3.3 to 5 feet (1 to 1.5 m)
Range: From Nigeria to Uganda and Zambia, with isolated populations in Mozambique, Tanzania, and South Africa
Habitat: Clearings in tropical forests, and plantations
Diet: Large and small mammals such as mice, rats, and small antelopes, as well as birds

FUN FACT
The Gaboon viper has fangs up to 2 inches (5 cm) long. These are the longest of any venomous snake.

PUFF ADDER *(BITIS ARIETANS)*

The puff adder is a large, heavy snake. Like other heavy-bodied snakes, the puff adder uses a form of movement called the caterpillar crawl. It moves on the ground in a straight line, driven by contractions of the muscles between the ribs. It is viviparous, usually producing litters of 20 to 60 young. The puff adder ranges between yellows, browns, and reds, with darker back-facing zigzags. The name refers to the remarkably loud hissing sound puff adders can make when threatened.

HOW TO SPOT

Length: 3 to 6.3 feet (0.9 to 1.9 m)
Range: Senegal to Somalia through South Africa; also southern Morocco, southwestern Arabian Peninsula, and Yemen
Habitat: Savannas, dry woodlands, and dry scrublands
Diet: Mammals, birds, lizards, snakes, frogs, and tortoises

VIPERS: NON-PIT VIPERS

RUSSELL'S VIPER *(DABOIA RUSSELII)*

Russell's viper is considered highly dangerous. It causes the most snakebites and deaths of any venomous snake in the world. It is especially common in rice paddies, where it can bite workers while they are harvesting. Untreated bites can be fatal. Russell's vipers are tan, brown, or deep yellow. They have a series of large dark-brown spots, each outlined in black, running along the body.

HOW TO SPOT

Length: 4 to 5.2 feet (1.2 to 1.6 m)

Range: South Asian countries, including India, Nepal, Pakistan, Sri Lanka, and Bangladesh

Habitat: Woodlands, scrublands, forest edges, grasslands, and human habitats, particularly rice paddies

Diet: Small mammals such as rats; juveniles feed on lizards

SAW-SCALED VIPER
(ECHIS CARINATUS)

Saw-scaled vipers are small but dangerous. They are highly nocturnal. People can be bitten when they walk near the snakes while barefoot. Untreated bites can be fatal to humans. Some populations of saw-scaled vipers lay eggs, while others bear live young. The snake is short and thick, with a broad, triangular head. It is brown or reddish brown, with an irregular zigzag pattern on the body and a plus-shaped pattern on the head.

HOW TO SPOT

Length: 1.6 to 2.6 feet (0.5 to 0.8 m)

Range: Widely distributed in southern and western Asia and Arabia

Habitat: Rocky valleys, hills, gravel plains, scrublands, and around old buildings

Diet: Small mammals, lizards, frogs, small snakes, and invertebrates, including scorpions

FUN FACT
The saw-scaled viper has scales that are serrated like a saw blade. They make a rasping noise when rubbed together as a warning.

VIPERS: PIT VIPERS

BUSHMASTER *(LACHESIS MUTA)*

The bushmaster is the largest venomous snake in the Western Hemisphere. It is also one of the deadliest. The bushmaster produces large amounts of highly toxic venom. Fortunately, this snake avoids confrontation. Its body is reddish brown to tan, with diamond-shaped markings down its back. The top of its head is black, and it has a sharp stripe just below each eye. The scales are heavily keeled, and there is a central ridge down the back.

HOW TO SPOT

Length: 6.6 to 11.8 feet (2 to 3.6 m)

Range: Entire Amazon Basin, Trinidad, the Guianas, and the Atlantic coast of Brazil

Habitat: Tropical lowlands and lower mountainous forests with high rainfall

Diet: Mammals such as rodents and opossums

FUN FACT

The bushmaster is unusual among vipers in that it lays eggs. It is one of few snakes in the world to guard its eggs.

COMMON LANCEHEAD
(BOTHROPS ATROX)

The common lancehead is highly venomous and is perhaps the most dangerous snake in its range. It is well camouflaged within its habitat. Lanceheads can be olive, brown, tan, gray, or yellow. Blotches on the back and sides may fuse to form bands. The underside is lighter. The lancehead is solitary and terrestrial. It often uses the ambush method to obtain prey, waiting until prey comes to it. Sometimes it actively forages for prey in leaf litter or even climbs trees.

HOW TO SPOT

Length: 4.3 to 5.9 feet (1.3 to 1.8 m)
Range: Venezuela, the Guianas, and the Amazon Basin, south to the foothills of the Andes Mountains
Habitat: Lowland tropical rain forests, forests around rivers, and farmlands
Diet: Mammals and birds; juveniles eat frogs and lizards

PIT VIPERS

The world's 150 pit viper species have heat-sensing pit organs on either side of their heads to sense prey. Nerves leading from the pits send signals to the same region of the brain that processes information from the eyes. The eyes sense images in the visible spectrum, but the pit organs sense heat. As a result, pit vipers actually have four eyes, with each set functioning differently.

VIPERS: PIT VIPERS

COPPERHEAD
(AGKISTRODON CONTORTRIX)

The copperhead is named for its head's coppery color. Like other pit vipers, its head is triangular. The body may be tan, copper, or gray, with hourglass-shaped patterns along the back and sides. The pattern offers exceptional camouflage for snakes waiting for prey among dead leaves on the forest floor. Copperheads are social and often stay near each other. During mating seasons, males are aggressive and may attack each other. In the winter, copperheads hibernate in dens with other copperheads, black rat snakes, and rattlesnakes.

FUN FACT
The tip of a baby copperhead's tail is lime green or yellow. It looks like a small worm or caterpillar, fooling prey into coming closer so the copperhead can attack.

HOW TO SPOT

Length: 2.6 to 4.6 feet (0.8 to 1.4 m)

Range: Southeastern and east-central United States to northeastern Mexico

Habitat: Rocky, wooded hillsides in dry oak woods or pine woods, often near water

Diet: Small mammals, birds, snakes, and lizards

EASTERN DIAMONDBACK RATTLESNAKE
(CROTALUS ADAMANTEUS)

The eastern diamondback rattlesnake is the largest rattlesnake. Because of its size, it can eat prey such as cats and rabbits. Its bite can quickly kill a human. The eastern diamondback swims well. It shelters in armadillo and gopher-tortoise burrows to avoid predators. It also gives birth to its young in these burrows. Eastern diamondback rattlesnakes are usually gray or light brown. A pattern of diamonds edged in white or yellow runs down the back.

HOW TO SPOT

Length: 3.3 to 7.9 feet (1 to 2.4 m)

Range: Southeastern United States

Habitat: Sand dunes, small stands of coastal trees, grasslands and woodlands at low elevations, and upland pine forests

Diet: Mammals as large as rabbits and cats, and birds as large as young turkeys

THE RATTLESNAKE'S RATTLE

A rattlesnake's rattle is made up of scales. These scales are loosely connected and make a sound when shaken. Each time a snake sheds its skin, it adds one segment to the rattle. Snakes shed multiple times a year, and rattles are easily broken. This means a person usually cannot use a snake's rattle to determine how old the snake is or how many times it has shed its skin.

VIPERS: PIT VIPERS

EYELASH VIPER
(BOTHRIECHIS SCHLEGELII)

The eyelash viper has bristly eyelash-like scales above its eyes. Its head is triangular. The eyelash viper's color varies from bright yellow to rusty orange to mottled greenish brown, depending on where it lives. This viper is active at night, hunting small vertebrates in the trees. It has been known to bite humans, sometimes fatally, and may occasionally eat other snakes. In keeping with its arboreal habitat, the snake is small and light.

HOW TO SPOT

Length: 2 to 2.6 feet (0.6 to 0.8 m)

Range: Southern Mexico, Central America, and South America

Habitat: Rain forests, especially close to water

Diet: Lizards, tree frogs, small mammals such as bats and mice, and sometimes sleeping birds

JUMPING PIT VIPER
(METLAPILCOATLUS NUMMIFER)

The jumping pit viper is short and stout, with a sharp ridge along its back. It is tan, light brown, or gray with dark-brown or black blotches. These may connect with spots on the sides, forming narrow crossbands. The top of the head is dark and the sides are lighter. The belly is whitish. Despite its name, this snake does not actually jump. When striking at its prey, it reaches out about half its body length, bites its prey, and hangs on.

HOW TO SPOT

Length: 1.5 to 2 feet (0.5 to 0.6 m)
Range: Mexico, from San Luis Potosi south to Oaxaca
Habitat: Rain forests and Atlantic slopes and lowlands
Diet: Mostly rodents for adults and insects and skinks for juveniles; they have been observed to eat other snakes

FUN FACT
In some parts of its range, the jumping pit viper is called *mano de piedra*, or "hand of stone." This refers to the intense swelling a person can suffer from a bite to the hand.

VIPERS: PIT VIPERS

NORTHERN COTTONMOUTH
(AGKISTRODON PISCIVORUS)

The northern cottonmouth is also called the water moccasin. It is closely related to the copperhead but is more venomous. Northern cottonmouths are aquatic snakes. The snake can be identified by the bright-white inside of its mouth, which it opens in defensive displays. Its body is pale gray or brown with darker saddles of the same color. In adults, the saddles fade and the snake appears more uniform in color.

HOW TO SPOT

Length: 3.3 to 5 feet (1 to 1.5 m)
Range: Southeastern, eastern, and central United States
Habitat: Slow-moving waters in warm areas, including rivers, lakes, swamps, and bayous, as well as moist land habitats near water
Diet: Mostly fish and frogs; also small mammals, birds, bird eggs, and reptiles

FUN FACT
The venomous northern cottonmouth has a thick, heavy body and a wide head. Nonvenomous water snakes are slender, with long, thin tails. Their heads are narrow and they lack distinct necks.

PYGMY RATTLESNAKE
(SISTRURUS MILIARIUS)

The pygmy rattlesnake is very small compared to other rattlesnakes. It produces a slight buzzing sound rather than a rattle. The pygmy rattlesnake's color varies by location. The snake can be black, tan, gray, brown, light red, or pink. It has alternating red and black stripes with black blotches between them. A black stripe runs from its eye to its mouth. When threatened, a pygmy rattlesnake slithers away if possible, but it will strike in extreme cases.

HOW TO SPOT

Length: 1.3 to 2 feet (0.4 to 0.6 m)

Range: Southeastern United States to Missouri, eastern Texas, and Oklahoma

Habitat: Typically moist areas with vegetation for cover, such as wet prairies, swamps, floodplains, forests, pastures, and lowlands

Diet: Small animals including frogs, snakes, lizards, and mammals such as mice

VIPERS: PIT VIPERS

SIDEWINDER (CROTALUS CERASTES)

The small sidewinder rattlesnake is highly adapted to desert life. Its sidewinding locomotion leaves a characteristic J-shaped pattern in the sand. Sidewinding allows the snake to easily move in sand. Sidewinders are small. In hot months they are nocturnal, spending daylight hours in rodent burrows or buried in the sand. The sidewinder's colors usually match its desert habitat. Sidewinders can be cream, tan, yellowish brown, pink, or gray with darker blotches on the back. The underside is white.

FUN FACT
Sidewinders are very similar to desert horned vipers in northern Africa. Their similarities in color, horn-like scales, movement, and even the texture of their scales are an example of parallel evolution.

HOW TO SPOT
Length: 1.6 to 2.6 feet (0.5 to 0.8 m)
Range: Southwestern United States and northwestern Mexico
Habitat: Sandy and rocky deserts, semideserts, and areas with scrubby, thorny bushes
Diet: Small mammals such as mice and kangaroo rats, lizards, and sometimes birds or other snakes

Sidewinding locomotion

TIMBER RATTLESNAKE
(CROTALUS HORRIDUS)

The timber rattlesnake is also called the canebrake rattlesnake. Its coloring and patterns vary depending on where it lives. Some populations are gray with black bands. Others are tan with yellow-brown bands. The timber rattlesnake can also have a brown stripe down the back. The timber rattlesnake produces only about nine young every three to five years. Young stay near their mother for one to two weeks and then disperse. Like other vipers, juveniles follow their mother's scent trail in the winter to hibernate in the same den.

HOW TO SPOT

Length: 3 to 5 feet (0.9 to 1.5 m)
Range: Eastern and southeastern United States
Habitat: Woodlands at higher elevations, and rocky hillsides with trees
Diet: Small birds and mammals

VIPERS: PIT VIPERS

WAGLER'S PIT VIPER
(TROPIDOLAEMUS WAGLERI)

Wagler's pit viper is a tropical snake. It once had a wide distribution. Because of deforestation, it is limited to unconnected patches of rain forest. Wagler's pit viper is a slow-moving, gentle species. It is highly arboreal. Females are longer and stouter than males. Males and juveniles are green with yellow bands. They have a red stripe through each eye. Females are black with yellow bands and green markings. They also have yellow on their faces.

FUN FACT
A Buddhist temple in Penang, Malaysia, is known as the Snake Temple. Wagler's pit vipers from the surrounding jungle shelter in the temple, which is now a tourist site.

Female

Male or juvenile

HOW TO SPOT

Length: Males 1.7 feet (0.5 m); females 3 feet (0.9 m)

Range: Southeast Asia including Thailand and Malaysia, the Indonesian island of Sumatra, and neighboring islands

Habitat: Tropical forests of the lowlands and coasts, and mangrove forests

Diet: Mostly birds and small mammals; juveniles feed on lizards and frogs

WESTERN DIAMONDBACK RATTLESNAKE *(CROTALUS ATROX)*

The western diamondback rattlesnake is one of several rattlesnakes in the southwestern United States. The snake is large and highly venomous. It can be gray, brown, reddish, or yellowish. It has a pattern of diamonds with white chevrons between them. The tail has distinct black and white rings. It has become rare in some areas, with many being killed in annual rattlesnake roundups. The western diamondback is aggressive. It stands its ground and may strike when threatened.

HOW TO SPOT

Length: 4 to 6 feet (1.2 to 1.8 m)
Range: Southwestern United States and northern Mexico
Habitat: Lowland floodplains, rocky canyons, wooded hillsides, semideserts, and farmlands
Diet: Birds, lizards, and small mammals as large as jackrabbits

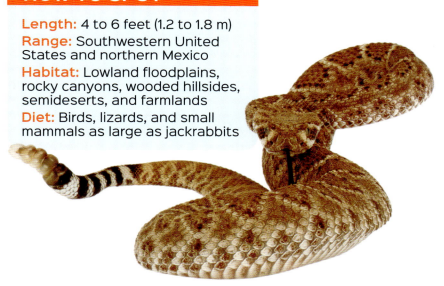

RATTLESNAKE ROUNDUPS

Snakes are often killed needlessly out of fear and cruelty. In rattlesnake roundups, tens of thousands of rattlesnakes per year are captured and killed. Hunters are paid for bringing in rattlesnakes. They often pour gasoline into tortoise dens to force out rattlesnakes. This pollutes the area and harms hundreds of other species.

TERRESTRIAL ELAPOIDS

AMAZONIAN CORAL SNAKE
(MICRURUS SPIXII)

The Amazonian coral snake has black, yellow or white, and red bands. Every scale is tipped in black. There are three black and two white bands between each pair of red bands. Most coral snakes are small and thin. But this species is remarkable in its very long length and its robust and powerful nature. Unlike many snakes, male Amazonian coral snakes are much larger than females. Amazonian coral snakes appear to use the massive nests of leaf-cutter ants as retreats. The snake is highly venomous.

FUN FACT
When a banded snake is moving quickly, the colors blend together to create the illusion of a fast-moving gray shape.

HOW TO SPOT
Length: 2.6 to 3.6 feet (0.8 to 1.1 m)
Range: Amazonian countries of South America
Habitat: Rain forests, forests near rivers, grasslands, and near human habitations
Diet: Lizards, caecilians (wormlike amphibians), and snakes, including pit vipers

BANDED KRAIT *(BUNGARUS FASCIATUS)*

The banded krait is large, dangerous, and easy to recognize. Its body is triangular in shape, rather than the cylindrical shape typical of most snakes. It has broad bands of alternating yellow and black. Its head is broad, flat, and black with arrow-like markings on the sides. It lives in termite mounds and rodent burrows near water. It can also be found near human habitats because of the presence of rodents. The banded krait is solitary and nocturnal.

HOW TO SPOT

Length: 5 to 7.4 feet (1.5 to 2.3 m)

Range: South and Southeast Asia, including India, China, Nepal, and various islands of Indonesia

Habitat: Coastal lowlands and low mountainous forests, swamps, and cultivated areas

Diet: Mostly snakes and eels, also lizards, frogs, small mammals, and fish

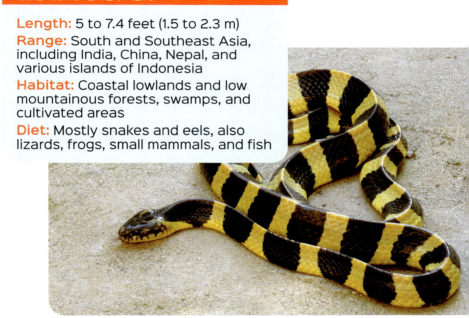

WHAT IS AN ELAPID?

Elapids are a large family of venomous snakes. Unlike in vipers, elapid fangs are fixed and do not rotate. They are much shorter as a result. Elapids deliver venom through these hollow fangs. Elapids include cobras, mambas, kraits, taipans, and sea snakes. Many, such as cobras, have a characteristic threat display. They rear up and spread the loose skin of their neck flaps, forming a hood.

TERRESTRIAL ELAPOIDS

BLACK MAMBA
(DENDROASPIS POLYLEPIS)

The black mamba is one of Africa's most feared snakes. Its body is dark gray or brown. When threatened, the black mamba flares out its hooded neck and opens its mouth wide, showing a black interior. It can deliver several bites very rapidly, delivering a deadly toxin. Without treatment, victims will stop breathing and die quickly. Although deadly, the black mamba is aggressive only when threatened.

FUN FACT The black mamba is one of the world's fastest snakes, clocking in at up to 12.5 miles per hour (20 km/h).

HOW TO SPOT

Length: 6.6 to 9.8 feet (2 to 3 m)

Range: Eastern and southern sub-Saharan Africa, with some sightings in western Africa

Habitat: Open, wooded habitats such as coastal bush, wooded savannas, and forests with rivers

Diet: Small mammals such as rats, squirrels, hyraxes, and elephant shrews; occasionally birds or other snakes

BLUE MALAYSIAN CORAL SNAKE *(CALLIOPHIS BIVIRGATUS)*

The blue Malaysian coral snake is long and slender. It has a blue or blue-black back. Its head, tail, and underside are bright red. It has lighter-blue stripes along the sides. The snake's venom glands behind the eyes extend one-third the length of its body. This means it can deliver a large amount of venom and is considered very dangerous. Usually the blue Malaysian coral snake flees when threatened. It can also bury its head in its coils and raise its red tail as a warning to potential predators.

HOW TO SPOT

Length: 3.3 to 6 feet (1 to 1.8 m)
Range: Southern Thailand, plus Indonesian islands of Borneo, Malaysia, Java, and Sumatra
Habitat: Rain forests in lowland and low mountainous areas, and farmland edges
Diet: Smaller snakes

TERRESTRIAL ELAPOIDS

DESERT DEATH ADDER
(ACANTHOPHIS PYRRHUS)

The desert death adder is red or orange with darker bands. This helps it camouflage into its various habitats. The snake is short with a thin, tapered tail. Its highly keeled scales capture morning dew, which the snake drinks. Its venom is highly toxic, but like many venomous snakes, it often gives a dry bite that lacks venom. These warning bites suggest that the snake can choose whether to release venom based on how dangerous a threat is.

FUN FACT
In another case of parallel evolution, this snake appears and behaves very similarly to many unrelated species of viper. Its name was chosen because of its remarkable similarity to the real adder from Europe.

HOW TO SPOT
Length: 1.3 to 2 feet (0.4 to 0.6 m)
Range: Much of Western and Central Australia
Habitat: Dry regions such as deserts, sand plains, and ridges; acacia scrublands, rocky flats, and outcrops
Diet: Small mammals and lizards such as skinks

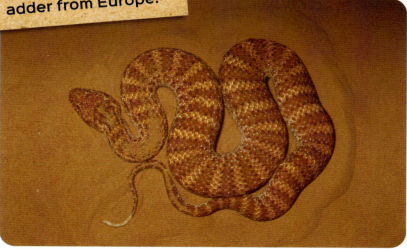

EASTERN BANDY-BANDY
(VERMICELLA ANNULATA)

The eastern bandy-bandy has alternating black and white bands. The snake has smooth scales, a rounded head and body, and a short tail. It is found in a wide range of habitats, from deserts to wet forests. The snake burrows and is nocturnal, often resting under rocks and logs. When threatened, it raises hoops of its body off the ground. The head and tail stay on the ground. Scientists believe this practice confuses predators and protects the snake's head. Because of this behavior, they are also called hoop snakes.

HOW TO SPOT

Length: 2 to 2.6 feet (0.6 to 0.8 m)
Range: Eastern and northeastern Australia
Habitat: Varied, from wet coastal forests to dry woodlands, grasslands, semideserts, and sandy deserts
Diet: Blind snakes

TERRESTRIAL ELAPOIDS

EASTERN CORAL SNAKE
(MICRURUS FULVIUS)

The eastern coral snake is small and secretive. It lives in dry environments but often comes out into the open after rain. Its bite is highly venomous. It has a black nose and a distinctive body pattern of red, yellow, and black rings. The yellow rings are narrow and touch both sides of the red rings. When threatened, the coral snake lifts its tail and curls the end of it.

HOW TO SPOT

Length: 2 to 2.6 feet (0.6 to 0.8 m)
Range: Southeastern United States
Habitat: Scrublands, live oak hammocks, flatwoods, and pinelands
Diet: Lizards, worm lizards, and small snakes, including other eastern coral snakes

RED, BLACK, AND YELLOW

In the United States, a rhyme is sometimes used to tell the difference between venomous coral snakes and their harmless mimics: "Red touch yellow, kill a fellow. Red touch black, venom lack" or "friend of Jack." But this rhyme only works for species in the United States, and even then it is not always accurate. Experts recommend that people forget about such folktales, avoid touching animals in general, and definitely avoid touching unfamiliar snakes.

EGYPTIAN COBRA (NAJA HAJE)

Cobras have elongated rib bones in the neck region. When they contract these ribs, the loose skin stretches and flattens, producing a hood. The Egyptian cobra is usually light brown with darker speckles on its back. Its hood is narrow, with a black band across the throat. In Morocco, the snake may be jet black. Unlike some other cobra species, the Egyptian cobra does not spray its venom. It bites its prey, delivering venom through its fangs. When challenged, it stands its ground and spreads its hood. The presence of rats and chickens attracts Egyptian cobras to human towns, where they often enter houses.

HOW TO SPOT

Length: 4.3 to 6 feet (1.3 to 1.8 m)
Range: Scattered populations around but not within the Sahara
Habitat: Dry woodlands, savannas, and semideserts
Diet: Small mammals, birds, bird eggs, snakes, and toads

FUN FACT
Egyptian cobra venom is used for medical research.

TERRESTRIAL ELAPOIDS

INDIAN COBRA *(NAJA NAJA)*

The Indian cobra varies in color. In India, it is typically all brown. In Sri Lanka, it may have bands. In Nepal and Pakistan, it may be all black. All Indian cobras have a characteristic hood marking called a spectacle. The marking looks somewhat like two eyes wearing glasses, or spectacles. This cobra is likely responsible for thousands of snakebite deaths each year. It is also highly important in ridding rice paddies of rats, which would destroy the crop.

FUN FACT
Buddhists believe the spectacle marking on the cobra's hood is the mark of the Buddha's two fingers, made after the cobra sheltered him from the rain.

HOW TO SPOT

Length: 3 to 7.3 feet (0.9 to 2.2 m)
Range: Most of India, plus Nepal, Pakistan, Bhutan, Bangladesh, and Sri Lanka
Habitat: Open areas, and woodlands and forests; common in rice paddies
Diet: Varied, including small mammals, birds, snakes, and amphibians

INLAND TAIPAN
(OXYURANUS MICROLEPIDOTUS)

The inland taipan is often called the fierce snake, but it is shy. It rarely encounters humans and has caused no known human deaths. However, it is often rated as the world's most venomous snake because of its highly toxic venom. The snake is large and brown, with darker edging on every scale. Head scales are either black-speckled or entirely black. The underside is yellowish. Inland taipans change color seasonally, becoming darker during the cooler months. Scientists believe this allows them to absorb heat more easily.

HOW TO SPOT

Length: 5 to 6.6 feet (1.5 to 2 m)
Range: A small region of east-central Australia
Habitat: River floodplains with black soil, and stony, open-desert plains
Diet: Mammals, especially rats

TERRESTRIAL ELAPOIDS

KING BROWN SNAKE
(PSEUDECHIS AUSTRALIS)

The king brown snake is also called the mulga snake. It lives in every terrestrial Australian environment, from desert to monsoon forest. It is large and stocky. Its color varies from yellowish brown to reddish brown, with lighter sides and belly. King brown snakes can be poisoned by the highly invasive cane toad. The toad is likely responsible for this snake's decline in northern Australia.

FUN FACT
The king brown snake appears immune to the venom of one of its prey species, the western brown snake.

HOW TO SPOT
Length: 3 to 5 feet (0.9 to 1.5 m)
Range: Most of the Australian continent, except for the extreme south and southeast
Habitat: Grasslands, woodlands, rain forests, and deserts, including semideserts
Diet: Mostly small mammals but also lizards and snakes; sometimes other king brown snakes

KING COBRA *(OPHIOPHAGUS HANNAH)*

The king cobra is black or brown with faint bands. The hood often has a pattern of chevrons. The female king cobra builds a nest of leaves to protect her eggs. This is unique behavior among snakes. She guards them fiercely against all threats. King cobra venom is less toxic than that of other cobras, but the king cobra releases enough venom in one bite to kill 20 people or one elephant.

FUN FACT
The king cobra is considered the world's longest venomous snake.

HOW TO SPOT

Length: 10 to 12 feet (3 to 3.7 m)
Range: Northeastern and southwestern India to southern China, Southeast Asia, the Philippines, and much of Indonesia
Habitat: Rain forests, mangrove swamps, and sometimes plantations
Diet: Primarily snakes; sometimes monitor lizards and mammals

THREATS TO THE KING COBRA

The king cobra is considered vulnerable to extinction. People kill these snakes out of fear. King cobras are also losing their habitats due to deforestation. Humans harvest the snake for food, skin, medicine, and the pet trade. India protects the species. The government captures king cobras and implants microchips to identify them if they are captured illegally.

TERRESTRIAL ELAPOIDS

MANY-BANDED KRAIT
(BUNGARUS MULTICINCTUS)

The many-banded krait is highly venomous. This snake is brown to bluish black, with a series of white or light-colored bands along its body and tail. This pattern is mimicked by many species of harmless wolf snakes. Its attraction to buildings and agricultural areas such as rice paddies makes it a constant danger to humans. It is typically a calm, timid snake, but it may be more defensive at night when it is most active. It feeds on many vertebrates but seems to prefer fish.

HOW TO SPOT

Length: 3.3 to 4.4 feet (1 to 1.3 m)
Range: Southern China, Laos, Vietnam, Taiwan, and Myanmar
Habitat: Low-lying wetlands, rice paddies, and near buildings
Diet: Snakes, lizards, small mammals, frogs, and fish

FUN FACT

Species of harmless wolf snakes have evolved to mimic the banded pattern of the highly venomous many-banded krait. This tends to scare off the wolf snakes' potential predators.

MOZAMBIQUE SPITTING COBRA
(NAJA MOSSAMBICA)

The Mozambique spitting cobra has greenish-brown scales with black skin, giving it a web-like appearance. Its underside is white, pinkish, or pale yellow with black on every scale. When its hood is up, a broad, black band is visible on its throat. This cobra is solitary and shelters in holes, crevices, and termite mounds. When confronted, it will rear up two-thirds of its length, show its hood, and "spit," or spray venom. It can also defend itself by biting or even pretending to be dead.

HOW TO SPOT

Length: 2.6 to 5 feet (0.8 to 1.5 m)
Range: Southeastern Africa, from Tanzania to South Africa to northeastern Namibia
Habitat: Wooded areas, coastal forests, savannas, and semideserts
Diet: Vertebrates, including small mammals, snakes, lizards, and toads

SPITTING COBRAS

Spitting cobras don't actually spit. They spray venom from their fangs. They squeeze the muscles on the venom glands, forcing the venom through front openings in the fangs. Some can spray venom up to 6.5 feet (2 m), causing scarring or permanent blindness in victims.

TERRESTRIAL ELAPOIDS

SAND RACER
(PSAMMOPHIS MOSSAMBICUS)

The sand racer is also called the olive grass snake or olive whip snake. It has an olive-brown back and a white or yellow underside. Its dorsal scales have dark edges. The snake is fast and often lifts the top third of its body off the ground when it moves. It covers its body with nasal-gland secretions, possibly to prevent drying out. Its venom is mild. It eats venomous snakes, including puff adders and black mambas.

HOW TO SPOT

Length: 2.6 to 6 feet (0.8 to 1.8 m)

Range: Sub-Saharan Africa, including Senegal, South Sudan, Kenya, and Tanzania, south to Namibia, Angola, Botswana, and South Africa

Habitat: Wet savannas, marshes, and forests at low elevations

Diet: Lizards, snakes (including venomous snakes), frogs, birds, and small mammals

FUN FACT
Sand racers are often mistaken for black mambas. But the sand racer is shiny, and the black mamba is not.

SONORAN CORAL SNAKE
(MICRUROIDES EURYXANTHUS)

The small, slender Sonoran coral snake has a black head followed by a white band. After this, it has bands that follow in a red, white, black, white, red pattern. Although highly venomous, the Sonoran coral snake is not very dangerous to humans. This is because of its small size and small mouth. When threatened, it lifts its tail and produces a popping sound. Scientists think the snake may force air out of its gut to make the sound.

HOW TO SPOT

Length: 1 to 1.8 feet (0.3 to 0.5 m)
Range: Southwestern United States and northwestern Mexico
Habitat: Dry, rocky, or sandy areas, including deserts, thorny scrublands, arroyos, and tropical dry forests
Diet: Various types of small snakes

TERRESTRIAL ELAPOIDS

STILETTO SNAKE
(ATRACTASPIS BIBRONII)

The stiletto snake is also called the southern burrowing asp. It is glossy black, brownish black, or purplish brown with a light underside. It has a pointed snout. When defending itself, the stiletto snake arches its neck and points its nose to the ground, trying to dig its head into the sand. It will press a spike on its tail into a person's hand if captured. It uses its long fangs to strike its victims horizontally, keeping its mouth closed.

HOW TO SPOT

Length: 1 to 1.6 feet (0.3 to 0.5 m)
Range: Southeastern and southern Africa, from Kenya to South Africa and west to Angola and Namibia
Habitat: Forests in low areas, wet savannas, grassy and shrubby areas, deserts, and semideserts
Diet: Shrews, mice, frogs, lizards, and small snakes

THE STILETTO SNAKE'S DAGGER

The stiletto snake's very long front fangs are hollow, mobile, and used independently. If the stiletto snake is held behind its head, it simply twists its head sideways, sticks one fang out through the side of the mouth, and jerks backward to bite the holder. It does this without opening its mouth. This fang anatomy enables the stiletto snake to inject venom into prey in tight spaces such as burrows.

TIGER SNAKE *(NOTECHIS SCUTATUS)*

The tiger snake is smooth with a large, rounded head. Some are solid brown, yellow, gray, or black. Others have broad bands, often yellow and black. Tiger snakes are viviparous. The tiger snake is greatly feared. Its venom is highly toxic, and it is aggressive if cornered. It raises its head and hisses, inflating and deflating its body. If the threat persists, the snake lashes out and bites.

FUN FACT
Population numbers of tiger snakes can be very high on offshore islands. Scientists are not sure why, but they believe few predators and lots of prey on these islands play a role.

HOW TO SPOT

Length: 3 to 5 feet (0.9 to 1.5 m)
Range: Southwestern and southeastern Australia, Tasmania, and other nearby islands
Habitat: Damp habitats, including rain forests, woodlands, floodplains, open shrubby areas, marshes, coastal dunes, and islands
Diet: Small mammals, birds, frogs, lizards, and snakes, including other tiger snakes

MARINE ELAPOIDS

BANDED SEA KRAIT
(LATICAUDA COLUBRINA)

The banded sea krait has regular bands of alternating bluish gray and black or dark gray. Its head is black on top, with two black stripes behind the eyes. It is sometimes called the yellow-lipped sea krait because of its yellow upper lip. Although venomous, it does not often bite humans, even when handled. It lives mostly in tropical coral reefs, but its specialized lung allows it to dive up to 197 feet (60 m) to find food.

FUN FACT
Banded sea kraits adapt how they move to their habitat. In the sea, they swim by moving their paddle-like tails back and forth. In sand, they use a sidewinding motion like desert snakes.

HOW TO SPOT

Length: 2.6 to 4.9 feet (0.8 to 1.5 m)

Range: Close to shore in the Indian and Pacific Oceans; Bangladesh to Japan; south to northern Australia; east to New Caledonia, New Zealand, the Solomon Islands, and Samoa

Habitat: Coral reefs, mangroves, and small islands

Diet: Fish, especially eels

ELEGANT SEA SNAKE
(HYDROPHIS ELEGANS)

The elegant sea snake has a black, olive, or gray head. The front half of its body is thin. The snake is yellow or gray with black rings. The back half of its body is much wider, and the black rings become oval saddles. There are black dots in the lighter spaces between saddles. The snake has a flat, paddle-shaped tail. It is highly venomous, and its bite can be fatal.

HOW TO SPOT

Length: 5.2 to 6.3 feet (1.6 to 1.9 m)
Range: Timor and Arafura Seas, and the ocean off eastern and western Australia
Habitat: Regions where fresh and salt waters meet and mix, including tidal creeks, estuaries, and river mouths over muddy or sandy bottoms; and in clear waters around coral reefs
Diet: Mostly eels

SEA KRAITS VS. SEA SNAKES

Sea kraits and sea snakes look similar, with distinct bands and flattened tails. But sea kraits are also at home on land. They mate, lay eggs, drink water, and digest food on land. Sea snakes live their entire lives in the ocean and give birth to live offspring.

MARINE ELAPOIDS

OLIVE-BROWN SEA SNAKE
(AIPYSURUS LAEVIS)

The olive-brown sea snake is named for its olive color. It has dark-brown or purple-brown markings on the back, and its underside is cream or yellow. It is one of the most common sea snakes on Australian coral reefs. It is highly adapted to life underwater, spending most of its time on shallow reef flats that are 32 to 131 feet (10 to 40 m) deep.

HOW TO SPOT

Length: 2.6 to 4 feet (0.8 to 1.2 m)
Range: Timor, Arafura, and Coral Seas around Australia and eastern Indonesia
Habitat: Coral reefs
Diet: A great variety of reef fish and shrimp

FUN FACT
The olive-brown sea snake can dive to 230 feet (70 m) and stay underwater for up to two hours before surfacing to breathe.

SHORT-NOSED SEA SNAKE
(AIPYSURUS APRAEFRONTALIS)

The short-nosed sea snake is dark brown or purplish brown with cream or olive-brown bands. Its head is small, short, and pointed, and its tail is flattened. Its venom is thought to be highly toxic. The snake is found on coral flats and in reef waters more than 33 feet (10 m) deep. Once fairly common, the short-nosed sea snake is now found only on two reefs off northern Western Australia. It is listed as critically endangered, and little is known about it.

HOW TO SPOT

Length: 1.6 to 2 feet (0.5 to 0.6 m)
Range: Ashmore and Hibernia reefs, possibly Western Australia coastline
Habitat: Coral reef flats in shallow water, and coral sand
Diet: Eels and other fish

MARINE ELAPOIDS

SMALL-HEADED SEA SNAKE
(HYDROPHIS GRACILIS)

The small-headed sea snake has an extremely small head and neck. This enables the snake to stick its head inside eel burrows on the ocean floor. Little is known about small-headed sea snake venom, but it probably has the high toxicity of other sea snakes. The small-headed sea snake's front half is much slimmer than its back half. Its body is light gray with darker gray bands, with the bands more pronounced at the head end.

HOW TO SPOT

Length: 3 to 3.3 feet (0.9 to 1 m)
Range: Persian Gulf to South China Sea
Habitat: Muddy deep-water bays and gulfs
Diet: Eels

FUN FACT
Sea snakes have a single lung that extends most of the length of the snake's body.

YELLOW-BELLIED SEA SNAKE
(PELAMIS PLATURUS)

The yellow-bellied sea snake is named for its bright-yellow sides and belly. A solid black stripe runs down its back. It has a very long head and tiny, nonoverlapping scales that help flatten its body for efficient swimming. The paddle-shaped tail has black spots or bars. While other sea snakes live in shallow-water reefs, yellow-bellied sea snakes are pelagic, living in the open ocean. They are the most widely distributed snake species in the world.

HOW TO SPOT

Length: 2.6 feet to 3 feet (0.8 to 0.9 m)

Range: Tropical and subtropical waters in the Indian and Pacific Oceans, from South Africa to the Americas

Habitat: Open ocean, especially where conflicting currents meet

Diet: Small pelagic fish

THE MOST PELAGIC SEA SNAKE

The yellow-bellied sea snake is highly adapted to its ocean lifestyle. It breathes through its skin. A salt gland under its tongue removes salt from ocean water. It uses its tail as a paddle, but it usually floats on ocean currents. Like many other sea snakes, yellow-bellied sea snakes drink fresh water that gathers at the surface of the ocean after heavy rains. Thousands of yellow-bellied sea snakes sometimes gather in debris where ocean currents come together.

GLOSSARY

arboreal
Primarily living in trees.

brackish
Slightly salty; a mixture of sea water and freshwater.

constriction
Squeezing or tightening; making something narrower by applying pressure.

endothermic
Able to regulate its body temperature internally; mammals are endothermic.

estuary
A partly enclosed water body where freshwater from a river meets and mixes with salt water from the ocean.

iridescent
Appearing to change colors in different lights or from different directions, like a soap bubble.

keeled
A type of snake scale that has a ridge along its length, giving the snake a rough look and feel rather than smooth.

mangrove
Trees or shrubs that grow on coasts in brackish water.

morph
A particular form of a species; for example, one morph may be a solid color while another is striped.

oviparous
Reproducing by laying eggs that later hatch.

prehensile
Capable of grasping, as a monkey's tail can grasp a tree branch.

rear-fanged
A rear-fanged snake delivers venom from solid or grooved fangs near the back of its mouth instead of hollow fangs at the front.

saddle
A marking that overlaps the back and continues down both sides of the snake, shaped like a horse's saddle.

viviparous
Reproducing by growing the young inside the body and then giving birth to live young.

TO LEARN MORE

FURTHER READINGS

Hale, K. A. *Essential Reptiles*. Abdo, 2022.

Starkey, Michael G. *Snakes for Kids: A Junior Scientist's Guide to Venom, Scales, and Life in the Wild*. Rockridge Press, 2020.

ONLINE RESOURCES

To learn more about snakes, please visit **abdobooklinks.com** or scan this QR code. These links are routinely monitored and updated to provide the most current information available.

PHOTO CREDITS

Cover Photos: Raja Seni/Shutterstock Images, front (boa constrictor); Eric Isselee/Shutterstock Images, front (Egyptian cobra), front (eyelash viper), back (California kingsnake); Sasin Tipchai/Shutterstock Images, front (corn snake); Ferdy Timmerman/Shutterstock Images, front (green vine snake); Vince Adam/Shutterstock Images, front (paradise flying snake); Barbara Ash/Shutterstock Images, front (ball python); Dwi Putra Stock/Shutterstock Images, front (Wagler's pit viper); Audrey Snider-Bell/Shutterstock Images, front (rattlesnake); Shutterstock Images, back (red-tailed pipe snake)

Interior Photos: Dwi Putra Stock/Shutterstock Images, 1 (reticulated python), 4 (top), 6 (bottom), 14, 18, 21, 82 (bottom); Alexander Sviridov/Shutterstock Images, 1 (garter snake), 40 (left); Shutterstock Images, 1 (cobra), 4 (bottom left), 12, 13, 15 (adult), 15 (juvenile), 23, 24, 25 (bottom), 32, 35 (bottom), 41, 49, 54 (top), 63, 65 (top), 67, 68 (bottom), 69, 70, 86 (bottom), 95 (top), 102, 112 (tree boa); Tino Anttila/Shutterstock Images, 1 (adder), 64, 112 (adder); Kurit Afshen/Shutterstock Images, 1 (Wagler's pit viper), 6 (top), 82 (top); Eric Isselee/Shutterstock Images, 4 (bottom middle), 4 (bottom right), 5 (top middle), 25 (top), 27, 66, 68 (top), 74, 76 (top), 81 (top), 91, 95 (bottom), 112 (cobra); DK Images/Science Source, 5 (top left), 37; Michiel de Wit/Shutterstock Images, 5 (top right), 40 (right); Dr. Morley Read/Shutterstock Images, 5 (bottom left), 53 (top), 59, 84; Stephen B. Goodwin/Shutterstock Images, 5 (bottom right), 52; Audrey Snider-Bell/Shutterstock Images, 7, 83, 112 (rattlesnake); Reality Images/Shutterstock Images, 8 (top), 61, 85, 92; Michael Benard/Shutterstock Images, 8 (bottom), 54 (bottom); Dan Koleska/Shutterstock Images, 9; Eugene Troskie/Shutterstock Images, 10; Larry Miller/Science Source, 11; Patrick K. Campbell/Shutterstock Images, 16, 50, 56, 72, 78 (top); Dwi Yulianto/Shutterstock Images, 17 (adults); Karl H. Switak/Science Source, 17 (juveniles), 88; Matt Jeppson/Shutterstock Images, 19, 26, 33, 36; iStockphoto, 20, 104; Jean-Paul Ferrero/Auscape International Pty Ltd./Alamy, 22; Scott Camazine/Science Source, 28; John Serrao/Science Source, 29, 79; Willem Van Zyl/Shutterstock Images, 30 (top);

NHPA/Photoshot/Science Source, 30 (bottom); Joseph T. Collins/Science Source, 31, 48; Marco Maggesi/Shutterstock Images, 34 (snake); Handies Peak/Shutterstock Images, 34 (Rod of Asclepius); Marian Cazacu/Shutterstock Images, 35 (top); Rowland Griffin, 38; Matthew L. Niemiller/Shutterstock Images, 39; E. R. Degginger/Science Source, 42; Rusty Dodson/Shutterstock Images, 43; Jason Patrick Ross/Shutterstock Images, 44; Randy Bjorklund/Shutterstock Images, 45; Nicholas Toh/Alamy, 46; Dwi Septiyana/iStockphoto, 47; Ferdy Timmerman/Shutterstock Images, 51, 60 (top), 60 (bottom); John Cancalosi/Alamy, 53 (bottom); Cesar Mayoral Halla/Biodiversidad Mesoamericana, 55; Froe Mic/iStockphoto, 57 (male); Stu Porter/Shutterstock Images, 57 (female), 97 (bottom); Ken Griffiths/Shutterstock Images, 58, 89, 93, 94; Agus Fitriyanto Suratno/Shutterstock Images, 62; Mark Kostich/Shutterstock Images, 65 (bottom); Dushan Muthunayake/Shutterstock Images, 71; Edvard Mizsei/Shutterstock Images, 73; Chase D'animulls/Shutterstock Images, 75 (top), 75 (bottom);
Roy H./Shutterstock Images, 76 (bottom); Rodolfo Ayala Plata/Shutterstock Images, 77; Tucker Heptinstall/Shutterstock Images, 78 (bottom); Chris Mattison/Nature PL/Science Source, 80; Joe McDonald/Shutterstock Images, 81 (bottom); Andre Coetzer/Shutterstock Images, 86 (top), 97 (top); Eng Wah Teo/Alamy, 87; Jay Ondreicka/Shutterstock Images, 90; Sam Yue/Alamy, 96; Jelger Herder/Buiten-Beeld/Alamy, 98; Nathan A. Shepard/Shutterstock Images, 99; Cormac Price/Shutterstock Images, 100; Gerry Pearce/Science Source, 101; NHPA/Photoshot/SuperStock, 103, 105; Kanishka D.B. Ukuwela/CalPhotos, 106; Auscape/Universal Images Group/Getty Images, 107 (top), 107 (bottom)

ABDOBOOKS.COM

Published by Abdo Publishing, a division of ABDO, PO Box 398166, Minneapolis, Minnesota 55439. Copyright © 2023 by Abdo Consulting Group, Inc. International copyrights reserved in all countries. No part of this book may be reproduced in any form without written permission from the publisher. Abdo Reference™ is a trademark and logo of Abdo Publishing.

052022
092022

THIS BOOK CONTAINS RECYCLED MATERIALS

Editor: Katharine Hale
Series Designer: Colleen McLaren
Content Consultant: Joseph R. Mendelson III, PhD; Director of Research, Zoo Atlanta; Adjunct Associate Professor, School of Biology, Georgia Institute of Technology

Library of Congress Control Number: 2021952333
Publisher's Cataloging-in-Publication Data
Names: Hand, Carol, author.
Title: Snakes / by Carol Hand
Description: Minneapolis, Minnesota: Abdo Publishing, 2023 | Series: Field guides | Includes online resources and index.
Identifiers: ISBN 9781532198823 (lib. bdg.) | ISBN 9781098272470 (ebook)
Subjects: LCSH: Snakes--Juvenile literature. | Reptiles--Juvenile literature. | Reptiles--Behavior—Juvenile literature. | Animals--Identification--Juvenile literature. | Zoology--Juvenile literature.
Classification: DDC 598.1--dc23